HOME BR [illegible] URES

Also by H. E. Bravery

SUCCESSFUL WINE MAKING AT HOME (Arc Books, Inc.)

HOME BREWING

WITHOUT FAILURES

H. E. Bravery

ARC BOOKS, INC.
New York

Published by ARC BOOKS, Inc., 219 Park Avenue South
New York. N.Y. 10003
Fifth Printing, 1970

Library of Congress Catalog Card Number: 66-19302
Printed in U.S.A.

Contents

Mead Making

Oh – Good Lord

The Horse and Mule live thirty years,
Yet know nothing of wines and beers.

Most Goats and Sheep at twenty die,
And have never tasted Scotch or Rye.

A Cow drinks water by the ton,
So at eighteen is mostly done.

The Dog in milk and water soaks,
And then in twelve short years he croaks.

Your Modest sober, bone-dry Hen,
Lays eggs for Nogs, then dies at Ten.

All Animals are strictly dry,
They sinless live and swiftly die.

But sinful, Ginful, beer soaked man,
Survives three score years and ten.

While some of us, though mighty few,
Stay sozzled till we're ninety-two.

Origin unknown.

Author's Special Note

This book is designed for all types of home brewers, from the veriest beginner with not the slightest idea where to begin to those with some experience looking for means to improve their product.

The complete beginner can begin by making some very excellent beers using readily prepared malt extracts and dried hops and only the simplest of utensils. The method is quick, straightforward and sure.

The beginner, when he has had some experience with the simple methods may then go on to tackle the slightly more advanced methods using grain malts and slightly more elaborate equipment. Those already experienced in making beers from malt extracts may go right ahead and use grain malts if they want to.

For the benefit of those who will want to use grain malts, I have included some details of the processes of the commercial brewer whom those using grain malts will be copying in every way. Using grain malts involves a period of mashing – as will be seen – and while this is a very simple process for amateurs willing to take some care in the process, those using malt extracts will not have this job to do, as a glance at the simple methods of making beers with malt extracts will show, chapter 4.

The lengthy discourse on commercial brewing is designed for those who will be using grain malts (so that they may see for themselves how closely they will be following the commercial brewer and to give them a clear understanding of the subject). Beginners using malt extracts need not bother to read this unless they want to from the interest point of view; for, strictly speaking, and because they are using the simplest methods, this does not concern them. It will, of course, when they decide they are ready to go in for making the very best of top-rate beers using grain malts.

This two-step method of learning is undoubtedly the best, for the experience gained in using malt extracts either in liquid or dried form readily obtainable from suppliers of home brewing equipment – Step One – allows them to go into using the slightly more elaborate methods involved in using grain malts – Step Two.

Step Three, if there really is one, is the stage when the operator, having used malt extracts and having advanced into using grain malts, decides to advance even further. Here he will use both grain malts and malt extracts in one brew, use his head in blending ingredients, evolve recipes of his own and perhaps methods as well; thus becoming an expert in his own right – and quite quickly. Such a man will make some extra super beers the like of which will not be obtainable elsewhere.

And when this stage is reached, there is no limit to the amount of blending of ingredients that can be carried out to obtain those special results that so often show a man up amongst his pals as someone exceptional. So, start with the simple methods and ingredients in chapter 3, and when you are ready, proceed to advanced aspects and you will be in for a lifetime's pleasant drinking with an absorbing interest into the bargain.

A Note About Measurements

The gallon measure used throughout this book is the British Imperial gallon. The U.S. gallon is approximately 1 pint less than the Imperial. In order to avoid reducing all ingredients by about one-eighth, the author suggests that the American reader simply add 1 extra pint of water to each U.S. gallon used. That is, if a recipe, for example, calls for 3 gallons of water, use 3 gallons *plus* 3 pints. All your measurements will then be correct.

Acknowledgement

I must here record my sincere thanks to the few friends who have helped me with my many experiments and the home brew supply firms for their generous samples. Also, I must thank the many readers of my various winemaking books who have sent me recipes for ales and beers. These have been tested, and the best of them are included in this book. It will please them to know that they have been invaluable assistance to me in producing the first comprehensive guide to home brewing of ales, beers, stouts and lager.

I

Before We Begin

Ales, beers, stouts, cider, mead, or any of the other alcoholic drinks detailed in this book are easy to make provided you understand not only why you are working in one particular way, but also why you must work in this way if you want the best results.

There are many methods for making every sort of alcoholic drink; some are good methods ensuring the top-most quality results, while others are so antiquated and slip-shod as to be quite comical. Others are half-way between the two. For far too long too many people have been following methods that can only result in disappointment. The methods here ensure success provided you know what you want before you begin. In saying this, I mean that you should have a good idea of what you want and then set out to make it as near to this as you can expect at first attempt.

In wine making we choose to make them sweet, medium or dry; light, medium or heavy. Naturally if the beginner winemaker dislikes dry wines and unwittingly makes them at first attempt, then it stands to reason that he will be disappointed. But if he had known what he was about he would have known he was making a dry wine and could have avoided what was to him a calamity because being a beginner he would not necessarily know how to rectify the fault when he had finished. It takes a little time and a few experiments before you can expect to turn out something exactly as you want it. And when you have done this, the experience gained, together with a bit of common sense, will show you how to improve your product so that it quickly becomes the main and favourite drink of yourself and your friends.

Too many people chuckle apologetically when offering 'a little drop of something I made myself'. Heaven knows why, for it is those who feel they have something to apologize for who turn out the best stuff. Hundreds of times and all over the country I have had people offer me home-made wines, beers, ciders and meads as if they were offering me diluted strychnine and were apologizing for the suffering to come. Mostly they were top-rate wines and beers. It seems to me that someone thinks just because *he* made it it *can't* be much good. This attitude has its good point because a man like that is clearly anxious to improve his product. But provided *he* is satisfied I can see no reason for striving to improve it beyond improving it to suit himself even more. After all, as experienced operators will agree, striving to improve can be overdone to such an extent that the end product bears no resemblance to the original. The 'improved' product, then, is no longer what it was and the operator is disappointed.

The aim should be to find in as few experiments as possible the recipe which gives the results nearest your special liking and then vary slightly the ingredients in future brews. This can be done quite simply by increasing slightly the amount of 'this' and perhaps reducing slightly the amount of 'that' until you produce precisely what you are after.

Altering the amounts of ingredients may not be necessary, for you might well hit the alcoholic nail on the head first time – and I hope you do. Either way, you will get a lot of pleasure for a comparatively small outlay, for if your first attempts are not all you hoped for you will realize at once that you are on to a good thing, because before long your own brew at sixpence or eightpence a pint will be as good as your favourite commercial product at three bob a pint. If you are a draught-beer man it's easier and cheaper still.

Beer Making

2

Commercial Brewing

It stands to reason that if we want good beers we must follow as closely as possible the methods used by those who know how to make them best of all – the commercial brewers. Obviously we cannot possibly follow the commercial brewer through every process from growing the barley and hops to bottling the finished product, with gigantic machines handling two or three hundred bottles a minute. Nevertheless, we can follow him most of the way.

Firstly, we can by-pass two of the most highly-skilled operations by buying quite cheaply ready-to-use ingredients – the very same materials as used by the commercial brewer. Thereafter we can follow him very closely indeed. In fact, we might well be very tiny miniatures of the great man himself.

Naturally, the beginner lacks the skill and technical knowledge to start with, but he quickly acquires a very simple technique or 'knack' of knocking up some really first-class beers, and he does this consistently after a few initial experiments. If this is so; and if our beer making is going to be simple with good results assured, there would seem to be no need here for a lengthy discourse on some of the technicalities of commercial brewing. But there is. Anybody can make good beers, but I believe that if the whole process is understood you will be able to see how closely you are following 'the great man himself,' so that you can see for yourself the importance of the simple methods you will be using. That highly technical processes go on naturally and unseen during these processes need not be discussed here. The fact that they do go on, how and why they go on without you having much to do with it will be discussed later on.

It is a fact that beer making is a natural process, apart from the boiling which is necessary if wild yeasts and bacteria are to be prevented from spoiling the finished product. The changes that take place in the ingredients are natural changes; all we need do is to start them off. Boiling halts these changes and destroys the causes of spoiled beers. Adding yeast merely starts the processes in a liquor freed of the enemies of successful brewing.

The art in commercial brewing is in selecting the materials best suited to the types and varieties of ales and beers turned out by each particular brewer. Any drinker worth his salt will have a wide knowledge of the various ales, beers and stouts available in the houses of the various brewers. The fact that each differs is the result of careful blending of ingredients.

Quality is of the utmost importance. Therefore, brewery groups grow their own barley and hops and harvest and process them according to their needs or select the best from overseas. The body in beer comes from malt obtained from selected barley; hops add flavour, 'tang' and bitterness where this is required and, of course, preservative properties.

Yeast in itself adds nothing to beers, yet without it beer would not 'happen'. The action of yeast on sugar in the wort (prepared liquor) produces alcohol, without which the wort would remain wort and never become beer.

Sugar is essential if the yeast is to produce alcohol – this point is covered in more detail in the practical section. Invert sugar is used in all breweries, not because it contributes flavour or any effective properties to the finished product, but because it is more readily fermentable than other sugars.

Barley is grown extensively in this country and very often the finest barley in the world is produced here. The quality naturally depends on soil conditions and the weather – the latter being, as we all know well enough, somewhat unpredictable. For this reason a good deal of barley is imported from areas where the climate is more reliable and better suited to growing the very best regularly each season to offset the poor quality sometimes produced here. Thus the commercial brewer might well use, in addition to some grown here, barley from Egypt, California, Canada, and perhaps India as well as from Europe.

Barley is but a seed and, within its husk, like all seed, is the germ of new life with a plentiful supply of food for the young plant.

Barley and malted barley appear identical. Barley is hard – so hard that the miller uses stone to grind it. Malted barley on the other hand is easily cracked with the teeth to exude the soft sweetness which is malt.

Malting barley is a highly skilled operation bypassed by amateurs who buy ready malted barley or malt extract. In malting barley, the maltster brings about artificial growing conditions so that the seed reacts as if it had been sown in soil. These growing conditions are stopped when the maximum yield of malt can be expected. Firstly, the barley is heaped and watered until germination takes place and growth begins. He then spreads this on the malting floor and never takes his eyes off it, as it were. Warmth and moisture encourages growth of the shoot within the husk and also brings about digestive ferments which cause starches and other substances to change into malt. When the young shoot still within the husk is about three-quarters along the seed, the maximum malt yield is reached. At this stage further growth is halted by drying or lightly cooking in a kiln. Thus the all-important malt is kept within the husk. The mass of rootlets is then removed and the malted barley – or malt, as it is now called – is stored for use as required.

The fuller flavoured, darker coloured malts are obtained by higher temperatures than those destined for pale ales which are of the palest colour. Crystal malt is produced by gas-oven treatment. Some malts are roasted while others – brown malts in particular – are produced in kilns burning wood fires.

Using one malt alone or blending two or many in the mash tun is the skill by which the brewer produces the beers for which he is famed. And it is here, by experiment, that the home brewer can turn out something quite remarkable once he has gained a little experience from using the simple recipes and methods detailed in the practical section.

Hops were once described as a noxious weed and outlawed by royal decree, but without them beers as we know them today would not exist. They are easy to grow – indeed, my grandfather used to grow them in the same manner as runner beans. Many country pubs are festooned with hops during the season; it is from such as this that home wine makers on a visit to the country pinch a few for adding to wines which benefit from the addition of a hop or two.

The fully grown, pale green hop bears some resemblance to a pine cone except that it is less tapered and paper-soft instead of woody-hard.

Take a handful of freshly picked hops and the palms immediately become sticky or tacky. This is because essential oils and resins have developed in the cone, and it is at this stage, when the cone is 'ripe', that the hops are gathered, for it is now that the full flavour is reached. Now – or a little earlier – the hop pickers converge on the hop garden in their thousands. Whole families up sticks, as it were, and sally forth for three or four weeks' working holiday where they can be assured of a good time into the bargain.

The drying of hops is a skilled craft. The hops are spread over the cloth-covered porous floor of the drying kiln through which warm air is passed until sufficient moisture has been removed to ensure that the hops keep well. If too dry the flavour is spoiled; if not dry enough they could turn mouldy on storing. When suitably dry the hops are packed by presses and stored until required for use.

Brewing Operations

The first operation in commercial brewing is the milling of the malted barley. As with drying hops, and malting the barley, skill is required if the best results are to be obtained. The malted barley is milled so that it is hardly more than cracked. From the mill the malted crushed barley or 'grist' is conveyed to the mash tuns (our mash tun will be a two-gallon polythene pail, as we shall see later on). The mash tuns of the brewery are enormous copper-domed vessels, often holding many thousands of gallons. It is in these that the first great changes take place. The malt is fed into these and mixed with water – from now on called 'liquor' simply because in the brewery there is no such thing as water except the stuff they wash the floors with. Brewery liquor, then, and malt form the wort in the mash tun. This is brought to and maintained at a temperature suited to the particular enzyme whose action is required to take place first. It is then increased and increased again until the brewer is satisfied that the changes brought about by the various enzymes are complete. At this stage the wort is boiled. As soon as the malt is put in the mash tun and wetted, the process halted in the malting kiln recommences. Starch is converted to sugars by digestive ferments or by the enzyme action just mentioned. Temperature control during this stage is essential because certain enzymes work – bring about their changes – at temperatures that would destroy others. Underheating would merely leave certain enzymes inactive so that the desired changes would not take place – or only partly take place. Complete change by enzyme action is necessary if good beers are to be produced.

Conversion, and extraction of flavours and other essentials taking place in the mash tun take from four to six or even eight hours. When the wort has been run off the near-spent grain into the coppers for boiling, more hot brewery liquor (not water) is sprayed over the grain until the brewer is satisfied that he has obtained all the goodness he can get.

Next comes boiling. From the mash tuns the wort is run into coppers and boiled with hops. It is during this boiling that the character of the beer is 'fixed' – or decided – and the enzymes which bring about the desired changes in the mash tun are destroyed. If they were not destroyed they would merely continue the process of convertion until the wort became a tasteless and unpalatable mixture of brewery liquor, spent hops flavour and alcohol. Boiling is necessary not only to halt the enzyme action but also to destroy wild yeasts and bacteria by sterilizing. Wild yeasts and bacteria cause spoilage ferments; this point is discussed fully in the practical section (p. 50).

After boiling, the wort is cooled by refrigerating machinery to about 60°f. At this stage yeast is 'pitched' into the wort; and now the great transformation from murky, flat wort to bright, foaming beer begins. This is known as fermentation, the action of which is described under ACTION OF YEAST on page 45.

A few hops are added during the latter stages of fermentation to add extra tang and preservative properties – some of these having been lost during boiling.

Varieties of Beer

Whether it be ale, lager, stout, old ale, pale ale or just beer from the barrel – it, or they – are all beers. But this has not always been so. For centuries 'unhopped' beer – that is, beer made without hops – was known as ale. Only beer made with hops was known as beer. However, as time went on, hops found their way into all beers whether they were known as ales, beers, stouts or what have you. The real difference between the various beers comes in the treatment of the malted barley, the amount used in the various beers and the amount of hops used in each.

Pale ale is made with more hops than other beers and the malt used is of the highest quality pale variety. It may be sold as either draught or bottled beer. Light ales are a weaker version of pale ale. Mild ale – the popular draught beer – is made with darker malt. Stouts are made from the darker malts and with some roasted malt.

It will be seen that by blending the various malts and by either increasing the amount of hops used a wide variety of beers can be made from the two basic materials – malt and hops. From all this the reader will at once see that he has only to use his imagination and his palate to decide on how, after a few initial experiments using the various recipes, to alter slightly the amount of ingredient to produce a beer that will be the envy of his friends.

Careful blending of light and dark malts and increasing or reducing the amount of hops used will show readily enough in the variety of beer produced how each may be altered a little more until the operator has designed a recipe for a beer that will be the only one for him forever more.

My urging you to experiment does not suggest that you will be disappointed in your first effort. Indeed, you will most likely be delighted. I make the suggestion of experimenting in case amongst the many recipes there is not one that suits your palate – but I'm willing to bet there is.

3

Home Brewing

It is a fact that in an hour or so of your spare time once a week enough beer can be made to last an average drinker a fortnight. A four-gallon lot may be made in any kitchen and it takes only a moment or two to assess how long thirty-two pints of the best will last.

Home made beer is cheap – as has already been pointed out – but this does not mean that it is poor when compared with commercial products. On the contrary, many ales, stouts and such-like bought over the bar leave a lot to be desired. Once you have the easily-acquired skill you can make yours better than the stuff now costing more than it is worth. And you can learn by simple experiment how to make beers of all sorts which will really suit you rather than having to acquire the taste for some commercial product that has come your way owing to the merging of two brewery groups. The skill in making beers comes in learning how to make the very kind of beer you have been looking for. Therefore, I expect you may have to make several lots before you are able to say that 'this' is just what you have been looking for and that the recipe you used in *the* one for you.

This is how skill in home wine making is acquired. Too many novice wine makers make a batch of wine with fruit that has become available without giving a thought to what the wine will be like or whether they will like it or not. The fact that it *is* wine is all that seems to bother them. This sort of person would go to a wine merchant for a bottle of wine with not the faintest idea of what they wanted apart from it being a bottle of wine. No person with any sense would go into a pub not knowing what he wanted. Clearly, the home brewer must have a pretty good idea of what he wants before he begins and then choose the recipe most likely to produce it. If he does this he will very soon succeed at what must be one of the most interesting and rewarding home hobbies there can be.

No licence is needed today and although this is an absolute boon that will make home brewing as popular as home wine making – there being more than half a million wine makers in Britain alone – some operators who have been making beers without a licence for as long as they can remember confess that now they are not breaking the law half the fun has been knocked out of it for them. It would seem that the beer was just that much better because in making it they were breaking the law. I suppose there is something in that, for as a child I remember that apples pinched from other people's orchards always tasted better than our own.

Being able to make beers as strong as you wish should not be encouragement to make them stronger than need be. The amounts of sugar given in the recipes make for good strong beers, that is, beers with a comfortable percentage of alcohol. You can make them weaker or stronger as you wish by altering the amount of sugar accordingly. The table on page 39 will show you how much sugar to use to obtain a given percentage of alcohol. But over-strong beers should not be the aim of anybody simply because, if they are made too strong, they become malt and hop wines rather than beer and therefore too strong to be drunk by the pint or even half-pint. It is all very well to acquire a reputation for being able to knock up a knock-out drop, but if your friends are affected by strong beers as many people are – they roll up their sleeves and challenge perfectly innocent bystanders to a punch up – it would be better to make them at roughly the same strength as commercial beers. In any case, the flavour of over-strong beers is spoiled and they are no longer the long, cool, refreshing drinks one looks for in beers, but temper- and hangover-inducing shorts.

You will, naturally, choose the simplest form of beer making to start with; the method calling for the use of malt extract and hop extract. This method is becoming extremely popular amongst beginners and will continue to be so for a very long time with a vast number of home operators simply because the ingredients are ready to use and easy to handle. Very excellent beers are made with these materials which are, in effect, the same as malted barley and dried hops.

However, the more ambitious will want to use grain malt (malted barley) and dried hops, as the commercial brewer does. For this reason, recipes for using either ingredients are included; some calling for malt extract and hops extract; others calling for grain malt and dried hops. Using grain malt (malted barley) and dried hops does make for better beers, but this is a little more expensive. However, the expense – the little there is – should not bar you from going in for making the best possible beers.

Years ago, home wine makers put up with all sorts of disappointing liquors made from all sorts of unsuitable fruits and yeast and fermented them in anything but a fire bucket. Today, they are a fastidious lot insisting on the best ingredients, the best yeast and the most suitable utensils – and so they should. The result of this new outlook has been the complete transformation of the nature and quality of home-made wines. Years ago, hardly any home-made wine was worth drinking; yet today they are absolutely first-class products easily on a par with the best commercial wines.

So let us do as home winemakers have done and learn to make beers as good as those turned out by famous breweries.

UTENSILS AND APPARATUS

From reading the outline on commercial brewing it will be seen that we need a mash tun for conversion and extraction of the mash-malt and brewery liquor. For this we may use a two-gallon polythene pail. This is quite suitable for a four-gallon lot, as we can make the amount up to four gallons at a later stage, thus avoiding the use of a larger vessel. We shall also need a copper for boiling the wort – the strained mixture from the mash tun plus hops and any other additions. The copper may be an ordinary domestic boiler provided it holds two or three gallons comfortably. A galvanized copper (boiler) may be used provided no acid is added until the wort is poured into the fermentation vessel. Acid added earlier than this would react on the metal to produce unpleasant tastes and effects and even poisoning. A very large iron saucepan with a mottled blue lining or similar wash boiler would also be suitable. Even so, it would still be wise never to add acid until advised in the recipes. In this way risk of metal contamination is avoided. Lined vessels must not be chipped. Do not use enamel pails for boiling the wort as these often contain lead in the glaze; this can cause lead poisoning. For fermentation purposes a polythene dustbin bought especially for the purpose is ideal. Before using it stand it on a level surface and put in one gallon of water. Mark on the outside with suitable paint a line where this reaches. Then add another gallon and make another mark. Do this with a third, fourth and fifth gallon until you have a bin marked from bottom to top at gallon levels. This will avoid a lot of messing about later on when a recipe calls for making up to a certain level with water. See also alternative fermentation vessel – page 32.

In addition to the three essential items mentioned you will need a 50-watt immersion heater costing about $1.00. These are designed for tropical fish tanks and are used by home brewers to keep the mash in the mash tun at a suitable temperature. This saves the bother of trying to keep the mash at a given temperature over gas or other heat for hours on end. Power consumption by the immersion heater is negligible. Bear in mind that constant and correct temperature of the mash is of the utmost importance, as it is during this stage that enzyme action brings about the important changes already discussed. The heater already mentioned does this admirably when used with a two-gallon polythene pail.

The above are *essentials.* A specific gravity hydrometer is not essential, but you will make your brewing much more interesting and results more certain if you use one. When to use is included in the recipes.

How to use the hydrometer and what it is used for is fully explained on page 32. It is simplicity itself to use – indeed, most home wine makers use one as home knitters use knitting needles – so don't be afraid of it.

Barrels or storage jars are not needed. Far better to take the beer from the fermenting vessel directly into bottles. Quart bottles are best and these should be used when directed in the recipes.

Alternative fermentation vessel. Many operators making large quantities of wine use a thick polythene bag as a fermentation vessel. This may be used quite well for fermenting beers provided it has suitable support; an old barrel past its usefulness is ideal. Merely put the bag in this and fill with wort. Deep crocks or bread bins, or even round plywood flour bins, may be used. As the polythene acts as a lining, almost any vessel normally unsuitable for fermentation purposes may be used. Make certain that any container of this sort has no sharp edges, protruding nails or metal parts that might puncture the polythene bag; remember that when full of wort the pressure on such objects is considerable.

If a bag is used, the top may be gathered together and held in place by an elastic band. The gas formed will find an outlet for itself where the top is puckered.

When bottling time comes, the top may be undone, folded back over the rim of the container and the siphoning tube inserted. One drawback with this type of container is that top-fermenting yeast sticks to it, but this is easily cleaned off. Whereas bottom fermenting yeast settles and works from the bottom, top-fermenting kinds rise to form a nobbly pancake on the surface. This should be scooped off daily if large amounts of yeast are made in a short time. Sometimes, if this 'cake' is left on the surface, it turns an unpleasant brown colour. This is quite natural and even if left undisturbed until all fermentation has ceased and then scooped off it will do no harm to the beer.

Here it is important to mention that fermentation vessels must be large enough to hold all the wort and to leave space for a good yeast head to form. If it is not big enough, the yeast will overflow, making a terrible mess.

Suitable polythene bags are best obtained from home brew supply firms, as these can be relied upon to be of true polythene and to be sound in seams and texture and of suitable gauge-thickness.

Using a Thermometer

Hardware stores, drug stores, and the suppliers listed on P. 153 stock thermometers covering all ranges of readings. The range best for brewing is from about 5° to boiling; if it goes beyond boiling point it will not matter. Many operators brewing in the simplest fashion seem to manage without one, but it is best to have one handy as it means that temperatures may be checked as required and this checking results in far more accurate brewing which, in turn, makes for far better beers.

When you get your thermometer, take my tip and put it in cold water – all of it – and bring to the boil and hold there for about one minute. This will harden it so that when it is put into high temperature liquids it will not break. It is very probable that all this talk about using a thermometer and hydrometer gives the impression to beginners that home brewing is a highly technical and complicated business – nothing would be further from the truth. The fact is that in using these simple instruments you are making the job much more simple and much more certain. Without them – particularly the thermometer – disaster can overtake you in the early stages, but this would not become evident until much later on when you might discover that, owing to having had the wrong temperature at the wrong time, there is an immovable starch cloud or that the beer lacks flavour or perhaps has gone far more bitter than it should have done.

The hydrometer can, of course, be done without, but as explained in the section covering this instrument, using it makes for safe working, gives you details of how fermentation is progressing, and allows you at a glance to calculate how much sugar to add to give a certain percentage of alcohol.

So don't stint on these important items and don't for heaven's sake imagine this business to be complicated. When you have all the utensils and ingredients ready and have read through the details here once or twice, everything will become very clear and very simple to put into operation.

The Fermentation Lock

Beginners need not use a fermentation lock during the early days of beer making. But when they have had a bit of experience they may find it very useful – I do myself. Readers already making wines must forgive me for boring them by repeating details they already know about. In wine making we use a fermentation lock to ensure that the fermenting wine is kept safe from wild yeasts and bacteria and to cut off the air and oxygen supply so that the yeast, which must have oxygen, turns to the sugar for it, thus producing more alcohol than it would if it obtained oxygen from the atmosphere. It is a fact that high alcohol wines cannot be made without a fermentation lock.

In beer making we use a fermentation lock during the later stages of production and in order to keep the fermenting wort free of wild yeast and bacteria. We also use it so that we can put the fermenting beer into jars, thus freeing the fermentation vessel for another batch.

As will be seen, after three or four days, fermentation of the beer slows down; it is at this stage that it may be put into jars. If put into jars during the vigorous ferment, the yeast will be forced up through the lock to such an extent that you will have beery yeast all over the place.

But if the lock is fitted to jars filled to within four or five inches of the tops with slower fermenting beer, there will be no bother. Fermentation locks are supplied with bungs already fitted for about 2s. 6d. One, or maybe two is all the home brewer will need. Before fitting the lock as shown on page 154 rinse it in some of the sterilizing solution and then stand it on its bung downwards in a cup of the solution to make sure the cork is purified. It may then be fitted to the jar. A little of the solution is then poured in the open end or dropped in with an eye-drops dispenser. The gas being generated inside the jar will push the solution up to one side and bubbles will pass through. The solution closes up so quickly that airborne diseases are prevented from gaining access. The lock may be left in place until all fermentation has ceased or until you are satisfied that it has gone on long enough to leave the right amount of sugar left unfermented and the beer is ready for bottling. This, of course, depends on whether you are making draught beer, or are adding sugar to draught beer to produce a gaseous beer, or whether you are using a hydrometer to ascertain how much sugar is left unfermented. All this may seem to complicate matters, but as soon as you have made a few brews all this will fall neatly into the pattern of things.

Use of the Hydrometer

We use the hydrometer in brewing to ascertain how much sugar the wort contains and to find out how much has been used up. This enables those who will be bottling fermenting beers to do so when there is just the right amount of sugar left to give the beer the required gas and to make sure that there is not enough sugar left to give rise to so much fermentation that the bottles explode.

We might argue that if we add a pound of sugar we know how much we have added and therefore know how much the wort contains. But it must be remembered that enzyme action has converted starches to sugar, the amount depending on the amount of malt used. Sometimes other materials are added to give starches into the wort; in this case we have no means of knowing how much sugar the action of enzymes has produced. By using the hydrometer we are able to find out, though the beginner need not bother with it unless he wants to know for sure how much alcohol he has produced.

The beginner would do well to make a few brews without using the hydrometer at the start. But if he is making bottled beers by bottling the nearly-finished-fermenting beer, he must use it to be on the safe side.

Now let me explain how it is used. Water has the gravity of 1000, often written simply as 1. We use water and its gravity of 1000 as a comparison – to put it simply. Therefore, as compared with water, or having a specific gravity of – whatever the figure might be. Now any liquid thicker than water will have a specific gravity of above 1000. The figure above the 1000 in our case refers to the amount of sugar in the wort. Therefore if we start off with a specific gravity of 1070, it means that the sugar content of the wort registers 70 on the hydrometer. All we have to do is take a sample of the wort in a trial jar supplied with the hydrometer, or a lager glass if you have not a proper trial jar. Let the hydrometer slide into the sample so that it floats clear of the sides of the jar. Make sure there is enough sample to float the hydrometer. Stand the jar on a level surface and note at what figure the liquid cuts across the stem of the hydrometer. This will be the figure representing the sugar content.

Compare this figure with the table on page 39 and you will see at once how much alcohol will be produced from the sugar. If you decide you want a stronger or weaker beer, all you have to do is to either add more sugar to increase the reading or add water to reduce it. Bear in mind that the more sugar the wort contains the higher the hydrometer will float. The less it contains the lower it will sink. Thus, as the sugar is used up by the yeast from day to day, the lower the readings will be from day to day.

It is not likely that you will take day to day readings, but if you did the result would appear like this:

Initial gravity	1·050
After first day	1·045
After second day	1·040
After third day	1·030
After fourth day	1·025
After fifth day	1·020

At this stage, fermentation will begin to slow down so that the reading will drop by only one or two degrees a day. When the reading has finally dropped to 1·005 it is safe to bottle the still-fermenting beer. A reading as high as 1·008 is sometimes safe, but beginners would be wise to bottle their beers when the reading is 1·005 as sometimes unforeseen factors give rise to more gas being produced than expected. As their experience grows, and if they decide they want more gas, they can bottle when the reading is 1·006 or 1·007.

Note. I must mention so that confusion is avoided that readings as I have shown them are often written without the decimal point and appear thus 1006 instead of 1·006 or 1007 instead of 1·007. Don't let this bother you if you happen to come across this elsewhere, as the figures mean the same whichever way they are written.

Specific Gravity and Alcohol Table for Beers

Having taken the hydrometer reading you will see at once how much alcohol will be made by comparing the reading (specific gravity) with its potential alcohol by volume. To increase the reading add 2¼ oz. of sugar for each increase of 5° you require: i.e. 4½ oz. for an increase of 10° and 6¼ oz. for an increase of 15° and so on.

Specific Gravity	Potential Alcohol by Volume
1·030	2·9
1·040	4·6
1·050	6·0
1·060	7·6
1·070	9·2

There is no need to go above these figures as 9% of alcohol is plenty for beers. The illustration on page 156 shows the hydrometer in a sample and registering a reading of 1·035.

INGREDIENTS

These are readily obtainable from the many home wine and home brew supply firms listed at the end of this book. Convenient sizes of all containers make purchase and measure easy and inexpensive. Indeed, whether you have a gallon or a hundred gallons on your mind, you are catered for.

Malt extract is malt extracted from the grain.

Hops extract is an extract of hops. *Dried hops* are dried hops, while *malt* is malt in the grain, or grain malt. This has to be cracked before infusion – before it is put into the brewery liquor in the mash tun. Such ready-to-use ingredients makes for trouble-free and easy brewing, and no one will blame you if you stick to using the readily prepared stuff. However there will always be those who will like to malt their own barley and perhaps roast it to obtain some special result. My grandfather used to do this and he produced results he swore could not be matched. He was a blacksmith in the spreading chestnut tree style with an immense capacity for home-brewed beer. In his day, home brewing was a laborious undertaking, but even with commercial beer at a penny a pint it was still economical to make it for oneself.

Sugar

A few years ago an argument started as to which sugar was best for making wines, and has gone on ever since; and I doubt whether it will ever be settled to the satisfaction of all concerned. Now that brewing strong beers has become legal the same argument will rear its head and fling the average operator into a quandary. He will feel that he simply must use the best possible sugar, or feel inadequate, or think that he is not going to make such good beers as can be made.

Can I settle the argument once and for all? No, I am afraid I cannot. The reason for this is simply that various sugars give slightly varying results. Each operator using a different sugar swears by that sugar; so, to him, that sugar is the best to use.

I have used all kinds of sugar, syrups and molasses in wine making. Let me say that sugars are different, though basically the same. For example, ordinary household sugar is two kinds of sugar in one, while invert sugar is the two sugars in household sugar separated from each other yet together in one mass when purchased.

Now, it is argued that invert sugar is the best for home brewing and that this should always be used. Yet when we add household sugar to the wort, the first action of the yeast is to invert the 'one' of household sugar to the two sugars of invert sugar – thus giving you invert sugar. The main argument is that if the yeast has to invert the sugar before it can use it for reproduction purposes, surely it would be better to give it invert sugar right away. But I cannot see the point in this – though I will admit that when invert sugar is added to the wort the vigour of fermentation is greater in less time than when household sugar is used. However, I find the difference in the end product – the finished beer – not nearly so great as many people would like to have me believe. A difference there is, but this is not likely to be noticed by the beginner who will not have experience to guide him. Therefore, beginners are advised to use household sugar for a time, at least, and then when they have sufficient experience to enable them to detect the differences in flavour the various sugars impart to their beers, they will be able to decide which sugar gives the flavour to their liking.

White invert sugar gives the same flavour as household sugar – otherwise no discernable flavour at all. Demerara does give flavour as well as some colour, dark brown invert sugars give a good deal of colour to beer and some strong and pleasing 'nutty' flavours. These flavours please some people, but not everybody likes them. Syrups – golden syrups, black treacle or green treacle may be used with other sugars to give special flavours, but experience is needed before you dabble with them – especially the strong-flavoured treacles. My mother used to make a treacle beer my father raved over – either in praise or because he drank too much of it; I never did find out. So it will be seen that using a little strongly flavoured treacle to impart a special flavour is worth trying out. However, as mentioned, you should use household sugar to start with and then when you feel like it use other sugar in place of it and then perhaps add a little strongly-flavoured syrup according to your own special tastes or wishes. It will be seen that some of the recipes include the use of sugars other than household sugar and that others include the use of syrups and treacles. You can, of course, go right ahead and use these if you want to, ignoring my advice above, and I doubt very much whether you will regret it. My advice is to use household sugar and to leave syrups alone for the time being is for those who feel that they would rather start off with a recipe that will produce a beer they are likely to be able to compare with their favourite at their 'local'. Beers made with other than household sugar or with the addition of syrups and treacles are, of course, first-class beers, but they are not, strictly speaking, near-identical to beers from public houses – at least, not from public houses in the area in which I live.

The chances are, of course, that when you have made beers with demerara sugar or other brown sugar with a little black treacle or golden syrup added, you will plump for these all the time and think it strange that I ever advised you to start off with household sugar and to leave the syrups alone.

Water

This is far more important than most people imagine. Indeed, breweries are famous because of the water supply they have (or did have before pollution ruined it), and upon the type of water supplied to your district depends to some extent the quality of your beer.

You may be quite satisfied with the beers you make regardless of the type of water in your area. However, to harden soft water and to soften hard water is quite a simple matter. Hard water is best for pale and bitter beers while soft water is better for mild ales and stouts.

If you are doubtful about the sort of water you have coming through your tap your local water board office will tell you whether it is hard or soft. You may then alter it to suit whichever type of beer you propose to make. Hard water may be softened by boiling before starting the brewing. That it will be boiled again during the process should be disregarded. A water softener has its advantages, but also its expense. Home brewing supply firms supply 'Burtonising' salts for treating all types of water very cheaply indeed and these do make a vast difference to the finished product, for they bring out the full flavour of the malt and hops. All water in the commercial brewery is treated in this fashion – hence their use of the word 'liquor' – brewery liquor, instead of water. Use the salts as directed by the supplier.

Do not imagine that you will be adulterating your water supply, you will merely be making good deficiencies; and, in any case, following the commercial brewer as closely as you can.

Colouring

Usually, this is not needed unless darkening of darker beer is needed or pale beers appear to be turning out too pale. Demerara sugar and other brown sugars if used will impart some colouring, as will brown invert sugar. These will affect the flavour to some extent, but many operators enjoy a reputation for the flavour given into their beers by the sugar they use. Where there must be no flavouring from the sugar and where darkening must be practised to satisfy a few operators' fastidiousness, then gravy browning may be used, but go easy with it. Burnt sugar may also be used. But where dark malts and black malts are used, colouring should not be necessary.

Sweetening

Some operators will want to sweeten their beers – especially their stouts. Obviously sweetening with sugar is going to give rise to more fermentation and therefore more gas than the bottles can hold. If sweetening is necessary use lactose. As with all other requirements this is obtainable very cheaply from home brew supply firms. Lactose will not ferment.

The rate to add will depend on the extent of the sweetness required. Some operators need only two ounces while others need four ounces to the gallon. Start off with two ounces per gallon and add more if necessary, rather than adding four ounces at the start and find you have made it too sweet.

FERMENTATION AND BOTTLING

The Action of Yeast

Choice of yeast is most important, for herein lies one of the secrets of successful beer making.

Many people obtain brewers' yeast from their local brewery and impart to some extent some of the characteristics of the beers turned out by that brewery. Others use dried yeast or bakers' yeast from doubtful sources, but don't do this yourself. Far better to get a good yeast from one of the suppliers listed at the end of this book, either top or bottom fermenting kind. Bottom fermenting yeast settles to the bottom of the fermenting vessel; most of this is left behind when the beer is bottled. Any in suspension at bottling time settles to the bottom of the bottles and sticks so hard that all but the merest trace of beer can be poured off clear before the yeast is disturbed.

Many home operators very successfully use yeast from bottled beers. They get a bottle of their favourite stout, or Schlitz or Budweiser and let it stand overnight. You then pour off the beer very carefully – not into the sink, of course, drink it! – leaving about an inch of beer in the bottle. This last inch will contain the variety of yeast used in the beer you have bought. This may be brought into activity by boiling about a quarter pint of water and about an ounce of sugar together. When this is cool pour into the bottle containing the yeast – using a funnel. Give a shaking, plug the neck of the bottle with cotton wool and in a day or two or perhaps even in a few hours, this little lot will be fermenting ready to add to the batch of beer you have been waiting to make.

When this batch of beer is nearly finished, you may take a little of the yeast from the top or bottom, treat it as above and you will have a new nucleus ferment ready to add to the next batch when advised in the recipes. You can do this each time you make a batch of beer.

The practice of using yeast from bottled beers can only be done successfully when the beers are dark; this is because only dark beers have a yeast deposit. Bright, light, sparkling ales do not have them.

By the time we add the yeast, sugar will already have been added to the wort in the fermenting vessel. In beer making we add enough sugar to give the amount of alcohol we want and bottle the beer at a point where there is very little sugar left. The fermentation that goes on after bottling charges the beer with the required gas – see draught or bottled beers: page 53.

Yeast feeding on the sugar produces alcohol and carbonic acid gas and turns the murky wort into clear foaming beer with a nice percentage of alcohol. The action of yeast has been fully described in various wine books of mine*; it is therefore enough

* SUCCESSFUL WINE MAKING AT HOME (Arc Books, Inc.)

merely to say here that it is the yeast that makes the beer for us, and to explain briefly what happens when yeast is put into the wort. Yeast is a living thing and like all living things it must reproduce itself if it is to survive. When put into a sugar solution – fruit juice in wine making, wort in beer making – it springs to life and almost at once begins to reproduce itself. In so doing it produces alcohol and the gas we see rising in the form of bubbles during fermentation. In wine making, fermentation goes on until so much alcohol is made that the yeast is destroyed by that alcohol. But in beer making we do not want nearly so much alcohol. Therefore, we add just enough sugar to produce the alcohol we want. In wine making we add from two to four pounds of sugar to the gallon. The yeast will use approximately 2½ lb. in producing about 14% of alcohol by volume. This amount of alcohol is usually sufficient to kill the yeast. Therefore any sugar in excess of 2½ lb. is left unfermented to sweeten the wine. Obviously, if we use only two pounds of sugar to the gallon the amount of alcohol will be less than 14% and the wine will be dry. The wine will be of 14% and still dry if 2½ lb. of sugar is used. If three pounds are used, the wine will still be of 14%, but less dry as there will be half a pound left unfermented to sweeten it.

I mention this to make clear that the more sugar you use the more alcohol you will obtain. But as mentioned, beers should not be too strong; indeed, the amount of sugar given in the recipes is plenty because the amount of alcohol produced from this is ample for beers.

During fermentation a good deal of frothing takes

place. This is yeast rising to the surface. Do not disturb unless advised in the recipes in the event of a top fermenting yeast being used.

Aids to Good Fermentation

Beer usually ferments well without much bother; indeed, a good vigorous ferment is assured if we proceed as advised. However, the yeast must have certain conditions if it is to make the alcohol we want without undue waste of time. The first essential to good fermentation is a temperature of about 65°f. and if this can be maintained, fermentation should be all over and done with in five to eight days. But sometimes we encounter a sluggish ferment and this is not a good thing if good beers are to result. Therefore, to ensure that the yeast will make good beers, give a little nutrient as used by home winemakers. This is merely a blend of chemicals essential to speedy yeast growth, they have no effect upon the taste of the finished beers.

Nutrient tablets used by winemakers are quite suitable for our purpose and should be used as directed by the supplier. This means, usually, merely crushing the tablet and dissolving the powder in a few drops of the wort and then stirring it into the rest.

A pinch of salt boiled with the hops, and a few crystals of citric acid per gallon will also assist fermentation. None of these additives will give their flavour into the finished beer.

Action of Enzymes

Little need be said about the action of enzymes, except that if temperatures during the mash tun and fermentation stages are not reasonably constant, enzyme action will not take place. Enzymes are biological catalysts; they bring about chemical changes essential in the production of good beers. Starches and other matter are converted to sugars, and flavour is produced; indeed, without their action we would not be able to make beers at all.

The temperature in the mash tun stage ensures that enzyme action takes place and a warm atmosphere during fermentation ensures that the yeast is happy. If too hot the yeast will be destroyed if too cold it will go dormant. Always allow the boiled wort to cool well – to about 70°f. if you have a thermometer – before adding the yeast and try to keep the fermenting beer at between 60° and 70°f. This will ensure a good ferment which is essential if good beers are to result.

Starch Test

It will be seen in the recipes that we must keep the wort at a certain temperature for a certain period. This is because during this period starches that would cloud the beer are converted by enzyme action into sugar which is later fermented out. It sometimes happens, no matter how careful we are, that not all the starch is converted during the time stipulated and it is not always possible by looking at the wort to decide whether or not the changes are complete. If conversion is not complete boiling will 'fix' the starch and removal later on will become a problem.

There is a simple test we can carry out to ascertain whether the changes have taken place or not at the end of the time given in the recipes. If changes are not complete the wort may be left for half an hour or an hour at the stipulated temperature until the changes are complete. Do not carry out this simple test until the end of the time given in the recipe, unless you feel sure that the changes have taken place earlier than expected.

Take about a tablespoonful of the wort into a glass or white cup or basin; to this add a few drops of medicinal iodine which has been diluted with an equal quantity of water. If the sample turns blue, starch is still present. If it does not, then the changes are complete. Do not worry if first tests show the presence of starch – just maintain the temperature for a little longer as already suggested and all will be well. A second test may be carried out if doubt still remains after extending the period in the mash tun.

Do not return tested sample to the bulk – throw it away.

The Causes of Spoilage

Readers of my various books on wine making will be familiar with the causes of spoiled wine and while we are not likely to encounter them in making beers, cider, meads and other alcoholic drinks detailed in this book, it is as well to know about them. We are then able to understand why precautions against them are so necessary.

Spoilage in meads and ciders, etc., is covered in their respective chapters. Here I am concerned only with spoilage in beers and how to prevent it. In beer making, risk of spoilage is quite remote. This is because any wild yeasts or bacteria on the ingredients are destroyed during the boiling of the wort.

Risks of contamination of the wort by yeasts and bacteria floating about in the air is also remote. This is because covering vessels as directed prevents them reaching the wort. If the vessels are *not* covered as directed, wild yeast and bacteria may reach the wort to turn it insipid and flat, oily or vinegary. Leave a bottle of beer or one with a drop left in the bottom opened for a few days and then smell it and the chances are that it will smell of vinegar. This is evidence that the vinegar bacteria has been at work on the alcohol and turned it to acetic acid – otherwise, vinegar. If this bacteria, or others or many of the wild yeasts in the air are allowed to come into contact with the beer, then calamity is in the offing.

Covering the Vessels

This is an elementary precaution almost anyone would take. But it is surprising how many would overlook the necessity. The mash tun (polythene pail), should be covered with a sheet of strong polythene with no holes in it. This should be tied down with strong string or, better still, a strong elastic band or several linked together and joined by a small wire clip or hook. This will hold the covering in place tightly so that air and airborne diseases cannot gain access.

The fermenting vessel must be covered in a similar fashion. The covering on this will billow up like a balloon under pressure from the gas generated. The gas will find an outlet for itself, keeping up a constant out-going stream to prevent diseases entering.

Sterilizing Bottles and Stoppers

All bottles and stoppers must be thoroughly washed in warm water. If, when bottles are held to light, evidence is seen of yeast stuck to the bottom or sides, they should be soaked in a medium-strength solution of water and domestic bleach, such as Brobat, for an hour or so. They should then be rinsed free of this with repeated doses of water. All bottles must in any case be treated with sulphur dioxide solution made up as follows. This is cheap, effective and ensures that any wild yeast or bacteria lurking in the bottles waiting to ruin your finished beer are destroyed.

Get 2 oz. of sodium metabisulphite, or potassium metabisulphite (there being two forms) from any chemist for about ninepence and dissolve this in half a gallon of warm water. Try to use a glass-stoppered bottle for this as it keeps better than in one with a cork. This is sulphur dioxide gas in solution. When bottle time comes along, half fill the first bottle, shake it up while stopping the neck with the thumb and then, using a funnel, pour into the next and then the next and so on. This half pint or pint will do a dozen bottles; afterwards, it may have lost its strength so throw it away. There is plenty left in the half-gallon jar to do several more dozen bottles. The stoppers should be soaked in enough to cover them for ten minutes or so.

Having sterilized the bottles they should be rinsed with boiled water that has cooled enough not to break them. Some writers on wine making assert that boiled water at this stage is not necessary, but it is, because water quite often contains wild yeasts which boiling destroys. The stoppers may be shaken free of the solution – no need to rinse them unless you want to. When bottling, I merely fill each bottle, take a stopper from the solution, give it one flick from the wrist and then screw it home.

Draught or Bottled Beers?

Any of the recipes may be made as draught beers, although all are designed for bottled beers with the use of the hydrometer. The difference between draught and bottled beer is that draught beer is flat in character (but not in taste), and bottled beers are gaseous or 'fizzy'. In making draught beers all we have to do is to allow fermentation to go on until the wort goes 'flat' – that is, when there is no longer any signs of yeast activity, no more frothing. This stage is usually reached in about eight days from the time fermentation began. Many beer types are of draught variety but all except draught bitter have a head on them when drawn from the barrel and served over the bar. This head – although it usually goes off very quickly – is most important from the appearance point of view, and that view only. I say this because the head itself adds nothing except an inviting appearance. The beer tastes the same after the head has vanished. In making draught beers we rarely get a head on them because no fermentation has gone on after bottling to give gas into the beer; and it is this gas produced by the ferment in the bottle which produces the froth or head we want. So, in draught beers made at home, there will be no head worth mentioning and if you are prepared to accept this then your draught beers can be first rate – except for the head. Heading liquid is obtainable from suppliers of home brewing materials; use this as directed and you will certainly get a first-class head, but it will add nothing but an appearance to the beer.

Draught beers may be put into tap-hole jars of whichever size is most suitable. I recommend the gallon size, as when some beer has been drawn off air is admitted. As soon as this happens, the beer begins to deteriorate. I do not mean that it will go off in a day or so. But as less and less is left in the jar, so the little remaining loses its character. If a gallon of beer is used in say, three or four days, the last pint out should be as good as the first one. But after a week, there would be a noticeable loss of quality in the last couple of pints. Obviously, where little is going to be used, the smaller the container the better. By all means use a two- or a four-gallon jar where there is going to be a lot of drinking in a short time. Tap-hole jars are particularly good for beers, as the yeast settles below the level of the tap and, apart from the first half-pint, which might come over cloudy, the rest may be drawn off beautifully clear.

Making draught beers is clearly the simplest form of home brewing and if tap-hole jars are not available use beer bottles kept for the purpose. Making bottled beers – gaseous or 'fizzy' beers – is the same as making draught beers except that either some sugar is left unfermented so that a little fermentation goes on inside the bottles to charge the beer with gas, or a draught beer is produced and a little sugar added at bottling time to give the re-fermentation required to charge the beer with the all-important gas. There is no point in adding sugar with the intention of producing gaseous beer if that beer is to be put into jars because as soon as the first pint is drawn off the gas will be lost – or most of it. Therefore, gaseous beers must be bottled and the best bottles to use are quart beer bottles with screw-stoppers or similar cider flagons – provided they are not clear-glass. All bottles for beers must be of brown glass, otherwise the colour and sometimes the quality of the beer will suffer. The directions in the recipes will produce gaseous beer, but if you want to make a draught beer into a gaseous beer you will have to add sugar and then put it into the type of bottles already mentioned. The rate to add the sugar is not more than three ounces to the gallon. This should be boiled in as little water as possible until dissolved and then mixed with the beer prior to bottling. Add this sugar when the beer has been siphoned off the yeast deposit; otherwise mixing it in will cloud the beer and a heavy deposit will form in each bottle. By using siphoned beer, there is much less yeast deposit, but still enough yeast in suspension in the clear beer to bring about the fermentation in the bottles.

Too much sugar added will give rise to too much fermentation so that the bottles, which can stand enormous pressure, will burst. If they do not when too much sugar has been added, the result will be an almighty geyser of foam and your precious beer will have to be licked off the ceiling.

Using the hydrometer reduces both risks; that of exploded bottles and accidental home decorating.

Good yeasts stick well to the bottom of the bottles so that all but the last dregs may be poured off without clouding the beer in the glass. This is not so important with dark beers as any cloud will be masked by the colour of the beer. It is with dark beers that the beginner should get his experience. Any yeast cloud will not impair the flavour of the beer; indeed, the heavy froth one sees on the top of most stouts and particularly Guinness – to which I am especially partial – is mostly yeast forced to the top of the glass by the gas rising. If you take a look at the bottom of an empty Guinness bottle you will almost always find some yeast lurking there. Certainly it does no harm; in fact, it is probably one of the most nourishing natural things next to mushrooms, which incidentally, are said to be the most nourishing thing known to man. Good yeasts do not impair the flavour, but baker's yeast and some dried yeast will give a bakehouse mustiness into the best of beers, and will in any case cloud the beer from top to bottom of the bottle simply because even if it does settle, the slightest disturbance will send it rising like smoke from a bonfire on a breezy evening. So use a good yeast that will stick to the bottom so that most of the beer may be poured off clear.

Trying to get a light ale or pale beer free of deposit can prove a problem. Firstly, if the beer is gaseous, there will inevitably be a deposit at the bottom of the bottle. This is because in allowing fermentation to go on in the bottles to produce the gas, yeast had to be present in the beer when it was bottled and this yeast reproducing itself produced more yeast. But as I have already mentioned, this yeast – provided it is a good one – will stick so that all but very little of the beer can be poured off without disturbing it. Pour carefully, inclining the bottle slowly, lowering the glass to meet it. If the quart bottles mentioned are used, the little beer left behind with the yeast, so that the yeast is not poured out as well, will not be missed. If only a pint of the quart is to be poured, far better to pour the quart into a jug so that the second pint may be drunk down in a little while. If one pint is poured and the bottle returned to upright, the yeast might stir up to cloud the whole of the remaining pint. A little practice and the application of a bit of common sense will soon show you how to get this problem settled to your satisfaction. But if you are as clumsy as some people cannot help being and simply do always disturb the yeast, serve your beer in a tankard or beer mug and you'll not know whether there is a yeast cloud in it or not.

How does the trade get the yeast out of clear ales? The fact is that they let them ferment right out, and then siphon the still beer (without gas) into bottles, or other containers and then charge them with gas. The word used is 'carbonated'. Maybe one day there will be a means by which any home operator will be able to do this; until then, the commercial brewer has the advantage over us.

Siphoning

It is always best to siphon beer into jars or bottles since in this way the heavy yeast deposit may be left in the fermenting vessel. If a lot of yeast passes into the bottles, as would happen if the murky wort were poured into bottles, a very heavy yeast deposit would form in them and, as we have seen, we do not want this.

Arrange the bulk beer on a table and the bottles on a lower level – a stool or on the floor. Insert the siphoning tube into the beer to a depth of a couple of inches or so. Suck the other end until the beer flows, pinch this end tightly and lower it into the first bottle and let the beer flow. Fill the bottle to within one and a half to two inches from the top, pinch the tube again and insert it into the next bottle and so on. As the level of the beer in the fermenting vessel falls, the tube may be lowered into it. If the beer falls below the end of the tube the siphon will be broken and you will have to lower the tube into the beer and suck again as you did in the first place. If the beer is draught beer or if you have checked with a hydrometer to ascertain the amount of sugar left unfermented the bottles may be stoppered at once and in the case of draught beer (non-gaseous), the bottles may be stored in a cool place. In the case of beers that are to ferment on in the bottles, the bottles should be kept in a warm place – not hot – for a few days and then moved to a cool place.

If you are making draught beer and at bottling time are proposing to make it into a gaseous beer, now is the time to do it. If this is what you are doing, then do not bottle from the fermenting vessel, but siphon off exactly one gallon and dissolve two and a quarter, or two and a half ounces of sugar in as little boiling water as can be used – about half a cupful – and pour this into the gallon. Stir a little to ensure dispersal and then bottle. This amount will produce enough fermentation to produce the gas required but not enough to burst the bottles.

Users of the hydrometer should bear in mind that two and a quarter ounces of sugar will raise the reading by 5°. So it will be seen that the amount of sugar mentioned above is just about the amount required without it being too much.

By treating the gallon we overcome the difficulty and riskiness of adding so much to each bottle – the amount having to be so small that it would be difficult to measure satisfactorily.

Don't forget to sterilize the siphoning tube, using the metabisulphite solution. Use proper siphoning tubing obtained from a home brew firm and get about six feet of it – it's very cheap.

Clarifying

As in wine making, clarifying beer should not be necessary as, if everything has gone according to plan, the beer will clarify itself in no time at all. However, it sometimes happens that everything does not go according to plan; we then have to resort to clarifying our beers. But do not attempt this unless the beer refuses to clear within three weeks after fermentation has ceased in the case of draught beers. In the case of bottled beer, the yeast should settle soon after bottling so that, held up to the light, the beer will be – or should be – as clear as a bell. As already mentioned, brilliant clarity as we want it in wines is not essential in dark beer and is not *absolutely* essential in ales of the light type that ordinarily one expects to see quite brilliant.

Isinglass is undoubtedly the best clarifying medium for beers. In treating draught beers, in jars, the best plan is to take a little of the beer – about a pint – and warm it. Into this stir about a teaspoonful of isinglass with a fork until it is dissolved, keeping the beer warm until this is affected. Do not let the sample become cold, otherwise it might gel –

turn to thin jelly. When all, or most, of the isinglass is dissolved, strain through fine muslin and pour into the bulk. Bung down again and in a day or so the beer will be brilliant.

Where gaseous bottled beers are to be treated a problem arises, for in opening the bottles the gas is lost. Therefore, in treating bottled gaseous beer you will have to return the lot to a large vessel and treat as for draught beers. Then, when it is brilliant, siphon the clear beer off the sediment into another large vessel and prime it again – add $2\frac{1}{4}$ oz. of sugar to the gallon and a speck of yeast (a very tiny amount). This will ensure that renewed fermentation goes on to give back to the beer the gas lost during treatment. After priming, the beer must be bottled as before and put away in the normal fashion.

Final Words Before You Begin

I find the best way to get the fullest value from the hops in these recipes is to boil them separately and in a small muslin bag with something such as a glass marble in the bag to submerge the hops at once. So bear this in mind when reading the direction, 'boil the hops . . .' Some loss of liquid will occur during boiling but this does not matter.

When straining the wort into the boiler and again when straining into the fermenting vessel, make sure the straining cloth is fine enough to hold back all solids. Coarse cloths of open texture should be folded several times before use.

If using the hydrometer to ascertain the gravity of the wort before fermentation so that you can arrive at the exact alcohol content of the beer when it has finished fermenting, take the reading when the wort has been made up to four gallons (or two gallons as the case may be) and when the sugar has dissolved. As the warmth of the wort will affect the volume and therefore the reading, it is better to let it cool and to take the reading immediately before adding the yeast.

It will be seen that there is more than one recipe for each type of beer: for example, there are two recipes for brown ale. Each recipe in this case and others makes for different sorts of brown ale, or bitter, or whatever it is.

And finally, do not expect to turn out at first attempt a beer exactly like the last one you tasted at your local – this would be expecting too much. Take your first shot at this as an initial experiment into finding the recipe which is going to prove the one to make the beer best suited to your personal taste. All tastes vary, therefore it is unlikely that the first recipe you use will be the one you will want to use next time. Bear this in mind and be prepared to experiment a little and I assure you it will be very soon that you make beer to surpass your expectations.

Note

In the recipes in the following chapters you will come across the reference: 'ferment for five-six days', or whatever it happens to be. This is a general purpose instruction meaning that under favourable conditions fermentation will have slowed down or be nearly complete so that hydrometer readings may be taken. They may be taken every day after the yeast has been added if this suits you. But it is at this five-six day stage that we must take note of the progress of fermentation so that we can work according to whichever type of beer we are making. If fermentation goes on longer than the days suggested, do not worry; it may go on for several days longer, even a week longer, depending on how even a temperature is maintained and whether this is in the 60°-70°f. range, as is best.

You will also come across the reference 'until the beer goes "flat"'. In using the word 'flat' I am describing the surface of the brew at the stage where fermentation has ceased. At this stage, when the yeast has been removed or where a bottom fermenting yeast is in use, the surface of the beer will indeed go flat; there will be no evidence of frothing or of bubbles breaking on the surface as we see the effect of drizzle-rain on a puddle. The beer does go flat in the sense that it is no longer lively – it does, in fact, become what it really is, draught beer. As already explained, this draught beer can be left as draught beer or primed to make it into a sparkling beer.

4

Simple Beer making and Using Malt Extracts

Malt extracts are obtainable from almost any chemist, but these are rarely suitable for our purpose. Do go to a reliable firm dealing in home brewing equipment, for these firms cater especially for us. Their malts and hops are of the finest quality and specially selected for our purpose.

Those who have read the parts in this book relating to the need for a mashing period to extract the maltose from the grain (p. 24) will understand that this mashing period is not needed with the recipes in this chapter because the malt extract we shall be using is the maltose we obtain by the mashing period. It is clear then that, simply speaking, the mashing has been carried out by someone else and we have the benefit of using the readily prepared ingredient. Only those using grain malts as detailed in chapter 5 will need to put the grain through a mashing period to extract the maltose.

It will be seen that all the recipes in this chapter are designed for two gallons. The fermentation vessel should hold more than this amount in order to allow for the yeast head that will form.

No large boiler is required, as the boiling can easily be done in two stages as in the recipes. Before

…gin using these simple recipes, do read the …ion detailing the causes of spoilage (p. 50) and …ake the necessary steps to avoid disappointment.

IMPORTANT NOTE: In all recipes, use one half ounce of yeast per gallon of beer.

LIGHT MILD ALE

2 lb. light dried malt extract
$\frac{1}{4}$ lb. caramelized malt extract · 2 oz. hops
1$\frac{1}{2}$ lb. demerara sugar
1 level teaspoonful citric acid
small level teaspoonful salt · yeast · nutrient

Boil hops and salt in about a quart of water for fifteen minutes. Take out the bag, squeeze when cool enough and pour hop-water into fermenting vessel. Add the malts, sugar and citric acid and make up to two gallons with boiling water – in two stages if your boiling utensil will not hold two gallons. Add nutrient, stir well to ensure malts and sugar are dissolved and then allow wort to cool to 65°-70°f. Add yeast, cover as directed and leave in a warm place for seven-eight days. If using hydrometer, take readings after five days until 1·005 is recorded and then bottle to produce sparkling beer. If hydrometer is not being used, allow fermentation to go on until beer goes 'flat' and then prime – add sugar to recommence fermentation – and then bottle. If draught beer of this sort is required, merely allow fermentation to go on until beer goes 'flat' and then bottle.

Pale Bitter

2½ lb. dried light malt extract · 4 oz. hops
2 lb. demerara or other brown sugar
2 pints strong freshly made tea
level teaspoonful citric acid
level teaspoonful salt · yeast · nutrient

Use four teaspoonfuls tea and allow to stand for five minutes.

Boil hops and salt in about a quart of water for fifteen minutes. Take out bag, squeeze when cool enough and pour hop-water into fermenting vessel. Add strained tea, malt, sugar and citric acid and make up to two gallons with boiling water. Stir well to ensure malts and sugar are dissolved and allow to cool to 65°-70°f. Then add yeast and nutrient. Cover as directed and leave to ferment in warm place for seven-eight days. If using hydrometer, take readings after six days until 1·005 is recorded and then bottle. If hydrometer is not in use, allow fermentation to go on until beer goes 'flat' and then prime – add sugar to recommence fermentation as directed – and then bottle. If draught beer of this sort is required, merely allow fermentation to go on until beer goes 'flat' and then bottle.

Mild Stout

1 lb. dried light malt extract
2½ lb. caramelized dried malt extract
2 lb. dark brown sugar
2 tablespoonfuls black treacle
level teaspoonful salt
level teaspoonful citric acid · 2 oz. hops
yeast · nutrient

Boil hops and salt in about a quart of water for fifteen minutes. Take out bag, squeeze when cool enough and pour hop-water into fermenting vessel.

Add malts, citric acid, sugar and treacle and make up to two gallons with boiling water. Stir well to ensure sugar and malts are dissolved and allow to cool to 65°-70°f. Add yeast, nutrient and cover as directed and leave to ferment in a warm place for six-eight days.

If using hydrometer, take readings after five days until 1·005 is recorded and then bottle. If hydrometer is not being used, allow fermentation to go on until beer goes 'flat' and then prime – add sugar to recommence fermentation as directed (p. 58) – and then bottle. If draught beer of this sort is needed, merely allow fermentation to go on until beer goes 'flat' and then bottle.

Strong Stout

1½ lb. dried light malt extract
2 lb. caramelized dried malt extract
2 lb. demerara or other dark sugar
4 tablespoonfuls black treacle
level teaspoonful salt
level teaspoonful citric acid
3 oz. hops · yeast · nutrient

Boil hops and salt for about fifteen minutes in a quart of water. Take out bag and squeeze when cool enough. Pour hop-water into fermentation vessel and add malts, sugar, treacle and citric acid. Make up to two gallons with boiling water.

Stir well to ensure malts, sugar and treacle are

dissolved and then allow to cool to 65°-70°f. Then add yeast and nutrient and leave to ferment in a warm place for seven-eight days.

If using hydrometer, take readings after six days until 1·005 is recorded and then bottle to produce sparkling beer. If hydrometer is not in use, allow fermentation to go on until beer becomes 'flat' and then prime – add sugar to recommence fermentation as already directed (p. 58) – and then bottle. If draught beer of this sort is wanted, merely allow fermentation to go on until beer becomes 'flat' and then bottle.

Light Lager

2½ lb. pale dried malt extract
2½ oz. hops · 1½ lb. sugar
¼ teaspoonful (level) citric acid · ½ teaspoonful salt · yeast · nutrient

Boil hops and salt for about fifteen minutes in a quart of water. Take out the bag, squeeze when cool enough and pour the hop-water into fermenting vessel. Add malt, sugar and citric acid and make up to two gallons with boiling water.

Stir well to ensure malt and sugar are dissolved and then allow to cool to 65°-70°f. Add yeast and nutrient, cover as directed and ferment in a warm place for five-six days. If using hydrometer, take readings after five days until 1·005 is recorded and then bottle. If hydrometer is not being used, allow fermentation to go on until beer goes 'flat' and then prime – add sugar to recommence fermentation and then bottle. If a draught beer of this sort is required, merely allow fermentation to go on until beer goes 'flat' and then bottle.

Continental Dark Beer

6 lb. dried light malt extract
1 oz. hops · ¼ lb. sugar
tablespoonful gravy browning
pinch salt · citric acid · yeast · nutrient

Boil hops and salt for fifteen minutes in a quart of water. Take out bag, squeeze when cool enough and put hop-water into fermenting vessel. Add malt, sugar and citric acid. Make up to two gallons with boiling water, stirring to ensure malt and sugar are dissolved. Stir in gravy browning. Cover as directed and leave to cool to 65°-70°f. Add yeast and nutrient and ferment in warm place for five-six days. If using hydrometer take readings after five days until 1·005 is recorded and then bottle. If hydrometer is not being used, allow fermentation to go on until beer goes 'flat' and then prime – add sugar to recommence fermentation as directed (p. 58) – and then bottle. If draught beer of this sort is required, merely allow fermentation to go on until beer goes 'flat' and bottle.

Brown Ale

1½ lb. dark malt extract · 2 lb. brown sugar
1½ oz. hops · ¼ oz. citric acid
small level teaspoonful salt
tablespoonful black treacle
2 liquorice sticks · yeast · nutrient

Note. Liquorice sticks add colour and desirable flavour and are available from most chemists at about 2d. each, otherwise obtain them from home brew supply firms.

Boil hops and salt in a quart of water for fifteen minutes, take out bag, squeeze when cool enough and pour hop water into fermenting vessel. Add malt, sugar, citric acid and black treacle and make up to two gallons all but a quart. While sugar and malt are dissolving, boil the liquorice sticks in the remaining quart of water and when dissolved add to the rest. Stir well to ensure malt and sugar are dissolved and allow wort to cool to 65°-70°f. Add yeast and nutrient. Cover as directed and leave to ferment in warm place for seven-eight days.

If using hydrometer, take readings after five days until 1·005 is recorded and then bottle. If hydrometer is not in use, allow beer to ferment on until it goes 'flat' and then prime – add sugar to restart fermentation, as already directed, and then bottle. This recipe ought to be made as a frothing beer, but if draught beer of this sort is required, merely allow fermentation to go on until beer goes 'flat' and then bottle.

Super Strong Ale

Best made as draught beer and drunk by the half pint. Best kept for grumpy relatives to induce them to sleep soundly while the rest of the household enjoys itself.

3 lb. dark malt extract
2½ lb. demerara sugar · 3 oz. hops
small level teaspoonful salt
¼ oz. citric acid · yeast · nutrient

Boil hops and salt in a quart of water for fifteen minutes. Take out bag and squeeze when cool enough. Pour strained hop-water into fermentation vessel and add sugar, malt and citric acid. Then make up to two gallons with boiling water. Allow to cool to 65°-70°f. and add yeast and nutrient.

Cover as directed and leave to ferment in warm place until beer goes 'flat' and then bottle.

5

Making Beers with Grain Malts

As will be seen, this chapter deals with a slightly more elaborate method of making beers than when malt extracts are being used. It is in using the following recipes that you will be following very closely the commercial brewer. Do not let this worry you. Just follow directions, but read first all I have had to say about commercial brewing; you will then understand why you are working in this fashion and why it is necessary to do so if good beers are to result.

Note. Do not forget to crack grain malts before use.

All the recipes in this chapter are designed to produce four gallons of beer – less the little that will inevitably be lost as deposit at various stages; so you should finish up with fifteen quart bottles of finished beer. The reason for working in four-gallon lots is that not only is the mash tun (polythene pail) most convenient in size, but also because the 50-watt heater recommended will keep this amount of mash at the required temperature at negligible power consumption. Later, when the mash is strained into the fermenting vessel and becomes wort and is made up to four gallons, the recommended fermenting vessel is also of ideal size.

However, there is nothing to prevent you making

two-gallon lots as initial experiments if you want to. But because the heater might make half the amount of mash too hot, you will have to start off with two gallons instead of one. The procedure when making two gallons would be as follows: reduce all ingredients by half. Put as much of the two gallons of water (liquor) as you can into the vessel with the ingredients. Then when this is strained, for boiling, the total amount of liquor can be made up to two gallons.

If you alter the amounts of ingredients to suit a special whim of your own bear in mind that

1. The more malt you use the more flavour and body you will obtain.
2. If more body is produced, more bitterness will be required to balance it to some extent.
3. Additional hops will produce this necessary bitterness.

MILD ALE

4 lb. crystal malt · 3 lb. demerara sugar
1 lb. flaked maize · 5 oz. hops
small level teaspoonful salt · $\frac{1}{4}$ oz. citric acid
dessertspoonful caramel

Bring seven quarts of water to 150°f., pour this into the polythene pail and add the malt and flaked maize at once. Put in the immersion heater, cover the vessel with polythene as directed and wrap the vessel in a blanket to conserve warmth. Switch on the heater and keep the mash at 145°-150°f. for seven to eight hours. At this stage you may try to starch test if you want to.

Strain the mash into the boiler and add two ounces of hops, the salt and caramel (gravy browning), and boil rapidly for one minute. Then simmer gently for forty minutes. Then add remaining hops and simmer for a further ten minutes.

Put the sugar and acid in the fermenting vessel and strain the mash on to it either through fine muslin or a nylon sieve. Stir well, making sure all sugar is dissolved, and then make up to four gallons with boiling water. Cover with sheet polythene and leave until cooled to 65°-70°f. Then add your yeast in whichever form you have it ready. Cover as already directed and leave in a warm place for seven-eight days. If top ferment yeast is used some skimming will be necessary. Cover again after skimming.

If using hydrometer, take readings until 1·005 is recorded and bottle as already directed. If draught beer is being made allow fermentation to finish and beer to go 'flat', and then bottle. If priming is being carried out (adding sugar to re-start fermentation), now is the time to do it.

Keep for three weeks in bottles.

Lager Beer – 1

4 lb. pale malt · 3½ lb. white sugar
3 oz. hops · small level teaspoonful salt
½ oz. citric acid · lager yeast · nutrient

Bring seven quarts water to 150°f. and pour into the polythene pail. Add the malt at once. Put in the immersion heater, cover the vessel with polythene and wrap the vessel in a blanket to conserve warmth.

Switch on the heater and leave for seven-eight hours. At this stage you may carry out the starch test if you want to. Strain the mash into the boiler, add two ounces of hops and the salt. Boil for one minute and then simmer for forty minutes. Add remaining hops and simmer for a further ten minutes.

Put the sugar and acid in the fermenting vessel and strain the mash on to it through fine muslin. Stir well, making sure all sugar is dissolved, and then make up to four gallons with boiling water.

Cover with sheet polythene and allow to cool to 65°-70°f. Then add the yeast. Cover as directed and leave in a warm place for eight-ten days. If using the hydrometer, take readings after six days and until 1·005 is recorded and then bottle as already directed.

If you are not using the hydrometer, allow beer to ferment out by leaving for a day or two longer or until the beer goes 'flat'. Then prime – add sugar to restart fermentation – as already explained (p. 58).

Keep for six weeks in bottles before using. This can, of course, be used sooner than this, but this lager is better for being kept a few weeks.

Lager Beer – 2

4 lb. pale malt · 2 lb. white sugar
1 lb. demerara sugar
2 tablespoonfuls black treacle · 3 oz. hops
1 small level teaspoonful salt
½ oz. citric acid · lager yeast · nutrient

Bring seven quarts water to 150°f. Pour into polythene pail and add the malt at once. Put in immersion heater, cover with sheet polythene as directed and wrap vessel in blanket to conserve warmth. Switch on heater and maintain mash at 145°-150°f. for eight hours. You may try the starch test at this stage if you want to.

Strain the mash into boiler and add the salt and two ounces of hops. Bring to boil and simmer for forty minutes. Add remaining hops and simmer for a further ten minutes.

Put both sugars, treacle and citric acid into the fermenting vessel and strain mash on to it through fine muslin. Make up to four gallons with boiling water and allow to cool to 65°-70°f. Add yeast and nutrient, cover with sheet polythene as directed and leave to ferment for six-eight days.

If using hydrometer, take readings after six days until 1·005 is recorded and then bottle. If hydrometer is not being used, merely allow fermentation to go on until beer becomes 'flat' and then prime – add sugar to recommence fermentation – and then bottle.

If draught beer of this sort is wanted, merely allow fermentation to go on until beer goes 'flat' and then bottle.

May be used a week or so after clearing, but better if kept for three weeks or more before being used.

Pale Ale – 1

2 lb. crystal malt · 2 lb. pale malt
5 lb sugar · 6 oz. hops
level teaspoonful salt · $\frac{1}{2}$ oz. citric acid
yeast · nutrient

Bring seven quarts water to 150°f. Pour this into polythene pail and add the malt at once. Cover the vessel with polythene as directed after inserting the immersion heater, and then wrap the vessel in a blanket to conserve warmth. Switch on the heater and leave for seven-eight hours. At this stage you may try the starch test if you want to.

Strain the mash into the boiler and add four ounces of hops. Boil for one minute and then simmer for forty minutes. Add the remaining hops and boil for a further ten minutes.

Put the sugar and acid in the fermenting vessel and strain the boiling mash on to it through fine muslin.

Stir well, making sure all sugar is dissolved and then make up to four gallons with boiling water.

Cover with sheet polythene as already directed and leave to cool to 65°-70°f. Then add the yeast. Cover again and leave in a warm place for seven or eight days.

If using the hydrometer, take readings after five days until 1·005 is recorded and bottle as already directed.

If not using hydrometer, allow fermentation to go on until beer goes 'flat', and then prime – add sugar to restart fermentation – as already explained (p. 58).

If draught beer of this sort is required, then no sugar is added. The beer when 'flat' is either bottled or put into tap-hole jars. But bear in mind what I have already written about the use of tap-hole jars (p. 54).

PALE ALE – 2

3 lb. pale malt · 1 lb. crystal malt
4 lb. demerara sugar · 1 lb. golden syrup
6 oz. hops · small level teaspoonful salt
½ oz. citric acid · yeast · nutrient

Bring seven quarts water to 150°f. Pour into polythene pail and add both malts at once. Put in immersion heater, cover with sheet polythene as directed and wrap the vessel in a blanket to conserve warmth. Switch on heater and maintain mash at 145°-150°f. for seven-eight hours. At this stage the starch test may be carried out if you want to try this.

Strain mash into boiler and add three ounces of hops and the salt. Boil rapidly for one minute and then simmer gently for forty minutes. Add remaining hops and simmer for a further ten minutes.

Put sugar, acid and golden syrup into fermenting vessel and strain the mash on to it through fine muslin. Stir well making sure all sugar is dissolved and then make up to four gallons with boiling water. Allow to cool to 65°-70°f, and then add yeast and nutrient.

Cover as directed and leave in a warm place for six-eight days.

If using hydrometer, take reading after six days until 1·005 is recorded and bottle as already directed (p. 57). If hydrometer is not in use, allow fermentation to go on until beer goes 'flat' and then prime – add sugar to restart fermentation as already directed (p. 58) – and then bottle. If draught beer of this sort is wanted then merely let the beer ferment on until it goes 'flat' and then bottle.

Keep in bottle at least one month before drinking – though it may be used sooner if required.

BROWN ALE – 1

4 lb. roasted malt · 1 lb. patent black malt
4 lb. demerara sugar · 4 oz. hops
1 level teaspoonful salt · ½ oz. citric acid
yeast · nutrient

Bring seven quarts water to 150°f. Pour this into the polythene pail and add the malts at once. Put in the immersion heater, cover with polythene as already directed and wrap the vessel in a blanket to conserve warmth. Switch on the heater and keep the mash at 145°-150°f. for seven-eight hours. At this stage you may carry out the starch test if you want to.

Strain the mash into the boiler and add 2 oz. hops, the salt (and a little colouring matter if you want to). Boil for one minute and then simmer for forty minutes. Then add remaining hops and simmer for a further ten minutes.

Put the sugar and acid in the fermenting vessel and strain the mash on to it, through fine muslin. Stir well, making sure sugar is dissolved and then make up to four gallons with boiling water. Cover as directed and leave to cool to 65°-70°f. Then add yeast and nutrient. Cover again and leave in a warm place for six-eight days.

If using hydrometer, take readings from five days or until 1·005 is recorded and bottle as directed. If hydrometer is not in use, allow fermentation to go on for a day or two longer until beer goes 'flat' and then prime – add sugar to restart fermentation as already explained (p. 58).

If draught beer of this sort is required, then when the beer has gone 'flat', it is merely bottled as directed without priming.

Drink after a week or two.

Brown Ale – 2

2 lb. roasted malt · 2 lb. patent black malt
4 lb. white sugar · 4 oz. hops
2 small level teaspoonfuls salt
½ oz. citric acid · yeast · nutrient

Bring seven quarts water to 150°f. Pour into polythene pail and add the malts at once. Put in immersion heater, cover vessel with sheet polythene as directed and wrap vessel in blanket to conserve warmth. Switch on heater and maintain mash at 145°-150°f. for seven-eight hours. At this stage you may carry out the starch test if you want to.

Strain mash into boiler and add the salt and two ounces of hops. Boil rapidly for one minute and then simmer for forty minutes. Add remaining hops and simmer for further ten minutes. Put sugar and citric acid in fermenting vessel and strain mash on to it through fine muslin. Stir well, making sure all sugar is dissolved and then make up to four gallons with boiling water. Allow to cool to 65°-70°f. Then add yeast and nutrient.

Cover with sheet polythene as already directed and leave to ferment for seven-eight days. If using hydrometer, take readings after six days until 1·005 is recorded and then bottle. If hydrometer is not being used, allow fermentation to go on until beer goes 'flat' and then prime – add sugar to recommence fermentation as already directed – and then bottle. If draught beer of this sort is required, merely allow fermentation to go on until beer goes 'flat' and then bottle. Keep for a few weeks to improve and clear, but may be used as soon as clear.

Stout

2 lb. patent black malt · 2 lb. crystal malt
1 lb. black treacle · 3 lb. white sugar
4 oz. hops · teaspoonful salt
1 oz. citric acid · yeast · nutrient

Bring seven quarts water to 150°f. Pour this into the polythene pail and add the malts at once. Put in the immersion heater, cover the vessel with polythene as directed and wrap in a blanket to conserve warmth. Switch on the heater and keep the mash at 145°-150°f. for eight hours. You may carry out the starch test at this stage if you want to.

Strain the mash into the boiler and add two ounces of hops and the salt. Boil rapidly for one minute and then simmer for forty minutes. Then add remaining hops and simmer for a further ten minutes.

Put the sugar, treacle and citric acid in the fermenting vessel and strain the mash on to it. Make up to four gallons with boiling water. Allow to cool to 65°-70°f. and then add yeast and nutrient. Cover as already directed and leave in a warm place for six-seven days.

If using hydrometer, take readings after five days until reading has dropped to 1·005 and then bottle as already advised. If hydrometer is not in use, allow fermentation to go on until stout goes 'flat', and then prime – add sugar to restart fermentation – and bottle. Some people like this as a draught stout; if you think you would like it, there will be no need to use the hydrometer or to prime the stout. Merely let it ferment right out and then bottle.

Note. Stouts are usually sweeter than ordinary ales and beers. If sweetening is needed, add a little lactose as already suggested (p. 44). This will improve after a few weeks in bottle, but may be used after two weeks.

Milk Stout

2 lb. patent black malt · 1 lb. pale malt
6 oz. flaked maize (cornflakes) · 3 oz. hops
2 lb. white sugar · 2 lb. powdered glucose
teaspoonful salt · $\frac{1}{4}$ oz. citric acid
yeast · nutrient

Bring seven quarts of water to 150°f. Pour into polythene pail and add the malts and flaked maize at once. Put in immersion heater, cover as directed with sheet polythene and wrap vessel with a blanket to conserve warmth. Switch on heater and keep the mash at 145°-150°f. for seven-eight hours. At this stage the starch test may be carried out if you wish.

Strain the mash into the boiler and add salt and two ounces of hops. Boil rapidly for one minute and then simmer for forty minutes. Add remaining hops and simmer for a further ten minutes.

Put the sugar, glucose and citric acid in the fermenting vessel and strain the mash on to it through fine muslin. Stir well, making sure all sugar is dissolved and make up to four gallons with boiling water.

Cover as directed and leave to cool to 65°-70°f. Then add yeast and nutrient and leave in a warm place for seven-eight days.

If using hydrometer take readings at five-six days until 1·005 is recorded and then bottle as directed. If hydrometer is not being used, allow stout to ferment out until it goes 'flat' and then prime – add sugar as directed to restart fermentation – and then bottle.

If a draught stout of this sort is required, merely let the stout ferment out until it goes 'flat' and then bottle.

Sweeten with lactose as required and keep in bottles for a few weeks or use as soon as required.

Oatmeal Stout

2 lb. black malt · 1 lb. pale malt · 6 oz. oatmeal
3 oz. hops · 4 lb. demerara sugar
small level teaspoonful salt
½ oz. citric acid · yeast · nutrient

Bring seven quarts water to 150°f. and pour into polythene pail and add malts and oatmeal at once. Put in immersion heater, cover as directed with sheet polythene, and wrap vessel with blanket to conserve warmth. Switch on heater and maintain mash at 145°-150°f. for seven-eight hours. At this stage the starch test may be carried out if you want to.

Strain the mash into boiler and add salt and two ounces hops. Boil rapidly for one minute and then simmer gently for forty minutes. Add remaining hops and simmer for a further ten minutes. Put sugar and citric acid in the fermenting vessel and strain the mash on to this, stirring to make sure all sugar is dissolved. Then make up to four gallons with boiling water. Allow to cool to 65°-70°f. and then add yeast and nutrient. Cover as directed and leave in a warm place for six-eight days.

If using hydrometer, take readings at six days until 1·005 is recorded and then bottle as directed. If hydrometer is not being used, allow stout to ferment on until it goes 'flat' and then prime – add sugar to restart fermentation – and then bottle.

If a draught beer of this sort is required, merely allow fermentation to go on until beer goes 'flat' and then bottle.

Sweeten as required with lactose. Keep for at least two weeks in bottles before drinking.

BRAVERY'S OWN STOUT

1 lb. roasted malt · 1 lb. black malt
2 lb. crystal malt · 3 lb. demerara sugar
1 lb. black treacle
½ lb. flaked maize (cornflakes) · 4 oz. hops
small level teaspoonful salt
½ oz. citric acid · yeast · nutrient

Bring seven quarts water to 150°f. Pour into polythene pail and add the malts and flaked maize at once. Put in the immersion heater, cover with sheet polythene and wrap vessel in blanket to conserve warmth. Switch on heater and keep mash at 145°-150°f. for seven-eight hours. If you want to try the starch test, now is the time to do it.

Strain mash into boiler, add two ounces of hops and the salt. Boil rapidly for one minute and then simmer gently for forty minutes. Add remaining hops and simmer for a further ten minutes. Put sugar, acid and treacle into fermenting vessel and strain the mash on to it, stirring until all sugar is dissolved. Then make up to four gallons with boiling water.

Cover with sheet polythene as directed and leave to cool to 65°-70°f. Then add yeast and nutrient. Cover again as directed and leave in a warm place for six days.

If using hydrometer take reading after six days until 1·005 is recorded and then bottle. If not using hydrometer, allow stout to ferment on until it goes 'flat'. Then prime – add sugar to restart fermentation as already directed – and then bottle.

If a draught stout of this sort is wanted then merely allow fermentation to go on until the stout has gone 'flat' and then bottle.

Keep for two to four weeks before drinking. If you must sweeten use lactose to taste as already directed, but I think you will prefer this without it being sweetened.

Bravery's Super Stout

2 lb. crystal malt · 2 lb. patent black malt
1 lb. black treacle · 3 lb. white sugar
3 oz. hops · 2 small level teaspoonfuls salt
½ oz. citric acid · yeast · nutrient

Bring seven quarts water to 150°f. Pour into polythene pail and add the malts at once. Put in immersion heater, cover vessel with sheet polythene as directed and wrap vessel in blanket to conserve warmth. Switch on heater and maintain mash at 145°-150°f. for eight hours. At this stage you may carry out starch test if you want to. Strain mash into boiler and add salt and two ounces hops. Bring to boil and simmer gently for forty minutes. Add remaining hops and simmer hard or boil for a further five minutes.

Put sugar, treacle and citric acid into the fermenting vessel and strain the mash on to it through fine muslin. Stir well, making sure all sugar is dissolved and make up to four gallons with boiling water.

Cover with sheet polythene as already directed (p. 51) and leave to cool to 65°-70°f. Add yeast and nutrient and leave to ferment for six-eight days.

If using hydrometer, take readings after five days until 1·005 is recorded and then bottle. If hydrometer is not being used, allow fermentation to go on until beer becomes 'flat' and then prime – add sugar to recommence fermentation – and then bottle. If draught beer of this sort is wanted merely bottle the beer when it has gone 'flat'. Improves with keeping for six or more weeks, though it may be used as soon as all yeast has settled and the beer is clear.

Bravery's Best Bitter

4 lb. crystal malt · 2 lb. golden syrup
2 lb. white sugar · 5 oz. hops
level teaspoonful salt · ¼ oz. citric acid
yeast · nutrient

Bring seven quarts water to 150°f. Pour this into polythene pail and add the malts at once. Put in immersion heater, cover with polythene and wrap vessel in a blanket to conserve warmth. Switch on heater and keep the wort at 145°-150°f. for seven-eight hours. At this stage you may try the starch test if you want to.

Strain into boiler and add three ounces of hops and the salt. Bring to boil for five minutes and then simmer gently for forty minutes. Add remaining hops and simmer for a further ten minutes. Put sugar, syrup and acid into the fermenting vessel and strain the mash on to it, stirring thoroughly until all sugar is dissolved. Make up to four gallons with boiling water, cover with sheet polythene and leave to cool to 65°-70°f. Then add yeast and nutrient. Cover as directed and leave in warm place for seven-eight days.

If using hydrometer, take readings after six days until 1·005 is recorded and then bottle as already directed. If hydrometer is not being used, let the beer ferment on until it goes 'flat' and then prime – add sugar to recommence fermentation – and then bottle. If a draught bitter is required – most bitters are of the draught variety – merely allow the beer to continue fermenting until it has gone 'flat' and then bottle.

May be used after ten days in bottle, but is better after three weeks.

6

Mock Beers

The recipes in this short chapter make what are popularly called 'mock beers', and that is precisely what they are. The fact that they are called beers at all is probably because they are too low in alcohol to be called wines and that where one recipe calls for the use of hops another needs some malt. In some recipes both malt and hops are used in smaller amounts than those used for true beers.

Like all aspects of home wine making and beer brewing, the making of mock beers is becoming more popular every day. Messing about in the cellar, kitchen or outhouse, knocking up all sorts of alcoholic drinks has taken such a hold on the country that I shall not be surprised to find a bottle of something fermenting under the seat of my train one morning, or to see a fermentation lock sticking out of my neighbour's brief case.

If the trend continues, and I can safely predict that it will because we are no longer working in the dark with only hearsay and near-witchcraft to guide us, there will be hardly a household in the country not making some sort of beverage from low alcohol beers to strong beers and high alcohol wines fit for royalty.

The type of yeast is not important in these recipes, but do not use fresh baker's yeast as this is likely to impart a 'yeasty' flavour, or bakehouse mustiness to the beer. A good dried yeast in granulated form is useful. Do not use expensive wine yeast as this would be wasteful because the characteristics imparted to wines by good quality wine yeasts would be lost in these beers.

Spruce Beer

Definitely a refresher beer.

2½ tablespoonsful spruce essence
1 lb. sugar · 1 lb. pale malt extract
⅛ oz. citric acid or juice of 1 lemon
yeast · nutrient · 2 gallons water

Put malt and sugar in boiler and add half a gallon of water, bring to boil and simmer for five minutes. Pour into fermenting vessel and add citric acid and spruce essence. Allow to cool to 65°-70°f. and add yeast and nutrient. Cover as directed for other beers and allow to ferment as for these. This is best made as draught beer, therefore merely allow fermentation to go on until beer goes 'flat', and then bottle.

Best if kept for at least two weeks.

Spruce essence is available from any chemist.

Nettle Beer

1 gallon young stinging nettle tops
2 oz. hops · ¼ oz. root ginger
2 lb. dark malt extract
1½ lb. demerara sugar
¼ oz. citric acid (or juice two lemons)
yeast · nutrient · 2 gallons water

Wash nettle tops and allow to drain for a few minutes. Put them into boiler with hops, malt and root ginger and boil for fifteen minutes. Put sugar and citric acid into fermenting vessel and strain the boiling liquid on to it, stirring until all sugar is dissolved.

Allow to cool to 65°-70°f. then add yeast and nutrient, cover as already directed and leave to ferment in the way recommended for other beers. This may be sparkling or of draught variety. For directions for making either way see beer recipes in other chapters (e.g. p. 64).

Hop Beer

3 oz. hops · 1½ lb. demerara sugar
1 tablespoonful black treacle
¼ oz. citric acid (or juice 2 lemons)
yeast · nutrient

Boil hops in a quart of water for fifteen minutes. Strain into fermenting vessel and add citric acid, sugar and treacle and make up to two gallons with boiling water, stirring till all dissolves. Allow to cool to 65°-70°f. and add yeast and nutrient.

Cover as directed for other beers and leave to ferment in the manner advised for these.

This beer may be made as a draught beer or sparkling variety. For directions for making either way see beer recipes in other chapters (e.g. p. 64).

Treacle Beer

2 oz. hops · 1 lb. black treacle
1 lb. white sugar · $\frac{7}{8}$ oz. citric acid
yeast · nutrient

Boil hops in quart water for fifteen minutes. Strain into fermenting vessel, and add citric acid, sugar and treacle and make up to two gallons with boiling water. Stir well to ensure sugar and treacle are dissolved and then allow to cool to 65°-70°f. Add yeast and nutrient, cover as directed for other beers and allow to ferment as advised for these. This may be made as either a sparkling or draught beer. For directions for making in either fashion see beer recipes in other chapters (e.g. p. 64).

Bran Ale

12 oz. bran · 2 oz. hops
$1\frac{1}{2}$ lb. demerara sugar
1 dessertspoonful black treacle
$\frac{1}{4}$ oz. citric acid · yeast · nutrient

Boil hops in a quart of water for fifteen minutes and strain into fermenting vessel. Boil bran for half an hour in half a gallon of water and allow to soak in the hot water after boiling for a further half hour. Strain into fermenting vessel and add treacle, sugar and citric acid. Make up to two gallons with boiling water, stirring until sugar and treacle are dissolved. Allow to cool to 65°-70°f. and then add yeast and nutrient.

Cover and allow to ferment as directed for other beers.

To make either sparkling or draught beer of bran ale, follow directions given for other beer (e.g. p. 64).

A Relic of the Past – The Ginger Beer Plant

Some years ago in the National Press there appeared a recipe for ginger beer made up by means of starting off a 'ginger beer plant'. Unfortunately, and quite by accident, my name became mixed up with it and I was inundated with requests for details for weeks afterwards. The general direction – not mine, of course – was to put a couple of ounces of yeast in a cup with warm water and some ginger until it began to ferment, or rather erupt like a volcano which it invariably did, spreading its yeasty lava over everything. The direction went on to explain that half of this was then made up to one gallon with sugar and water and the other half given away. This part of it seemed to be a sinister secret; if you did not give half away the rest would die – it would, naturally through lack of sugar or other yeast food. There still persists a rumour that this makes a drinkable drink – it doesn't.

My reason for writing about it here is that the appearance of this book is certain to revive in the memory of many readers what was known to them in their early days as: Californian Bees, Beastly Beer Organism, Bee Wine, Bee Wine Organism, or Ginger Beer Plant. And I want to forestall anyone hoping to start this off all over again in order to save them endless trouble and disappointment.

Oh, I don't doubt that forty and more years ago

the 'drink' made from this stuff was acceptable; so was home made soap and boot polish and knee-high lace-up boots for teenagers.

You may recall, many of you, those bottles of cloudy liquid with some sort of sludge deposit in the bottom arrayed along a window sill that got plenty of sunshine to keep the liquid warm – sunshine, incidentally is another relic of the past, but I cannot concern myself with that here. In these bottles was a 'mysterious' substance rising and falling and by some stretch of the imagination giving the impression of bees buzzing about – hence Bee Wine. The same – or a similar effect – is often seen in jars of fermenting wine during the vigorous fermentation stage and when the jar is moved. Clumps of yeast rise to the surface and fall back again and because they have become dislodged, the gas rising carries them up to the top, where the weight of the lumps forces them down again.

But the yeast employed in Bee Wine or the Ginger Beer Plant is a type which forms tapioca-like clumps. There are other sorts which science describes as associations of yeast and bacteria to give a consortium with a possible symbiotic association between its components. In other words, a balanced complex mixture of yeast and bacteria. My advice to anyone thinking of reviving this, if only for the sake of novelty, is to forget it.

With modern methods of making wines where top class results are assured and with home brewing taking hold again, also with success assured, surely there is no need to go chasing dreams of a forgotten age – especially since the dreams are likely to turn out as nightmares.

7

A Recent Experiment

I have come to the conclusion that France and the Frenchman do not know what good beer really is; certainly, they do not make the heavier beers as we know them here. If they do, I have been unlucky for I have never found what I would myself call really good beer.

But I suppose if they wanted beers as we drink them they could make them easily enough. Beers in France are more like thin lager and I have a suspicion – probably false – that some of them are produced from remnants of the grape crops. This suspicion was strengthened last summer while drinking in the shadow of the Arc de Triomphe, someone remarked that the beer was like thin aerated grape wine and pretty weak stuff at that. He even suggested the grapes might be the small green ones from a certain area. Knowing wines as I do, I suggested that perhaps batches of poor grapes might be used as a basic material or even that wine from a poor season might be diluted and then refermented with just enough malt and hops to make the beer that is quite popular over there.

All this set me thinking, and when I think something usually comes out of it – if only a headache. Anyway, I set out to make beers as I found them over there because I discovered that similar beers are now becoming popular here, especially with the ladies whom I am particularly anxious to please.

Following the continental seems the vogue, but I am not jumping on their waggon for the sake of fashion. I believe that if we can all gain from copying, or attempting to produce a product popular elsewhere, it is a good thing.

One practice I hope will not catch on over here is that of wiping the head off freshly poured beer with, above all things, a lolly stick. In Paris, Lyons, Dijon, Marseilles, Toulon – everywhere we went the barkeeper dutifully performed this deplorable act. My French being better than my Russian it needed only half an hour of gesticulating to make clear that the English do not like their beers guillotined.

Back to the idea. I did not get precisely what I was after, but I did get close to it. As any winemaker knows, four pounds of grapes makes a very poor wine, but four pounds of grapes added to a wort at the stage where the yeast is to be added makes a vast improvement to the lighter ales and lager type beers. Not everybody will like this, so experiment only with a small batch where, if you are not pleased with the result, it will not be a calamity. A friend, with whom I work in almost everything I do in this line, made an excellent lager type beer. 1 lb. of pale malt extract, 1 oz. hops, 1 lb. sugar, 2 lb. of small outdoor ripened green grapes, one gallon of water, yeast and nutrient was all he used. He reached the stage where the yeast is added using the same method as that described in the chapter calling for the use of malt extracts (p. 63) and added the crushed grapes. These he strained out after five days, and allowed fermentation to go on until the hydrometer recorded 1·005. He then bottled the lager and kept it for three months. Not being fond of lager of any sort, I was not a judge of the final product, but others were quite thrilled with it. No acid was added because the grapes added enough.

My own efforts have pleased others more than me – but only because I am not fond of lager types. Wine makers are bound to ask, would concentrated grape juice be suitable for such an experiment? I have used a white concentrate – one pint to the four gallon batch of a light ale and lager recipe with some success. Oh, I can hear the die-hard wine lovers accusing me of trying to make winey beer or beery wine and wondering why I cannot stick to one or the other. But if the end product is a pleasure to a number of people the wrath of the few will lie lightly upon my shoulders. I like beer – very much. I also like wines – very much. Anything midway between the two would not, I am sure, be pleasant. These lager types made with a few added grapes are not midway between wine and beer; they are something quite unique.

If you try something of this sort, use only the juice of black grapes otherwise you will have a pink lager owing to the colour coming from the grape skins. Pink Lager – well, why not? The die-hards will be at my throat for this one!

Other trials I carried out – readers of my various wine books will know I'm a devil for experimenting – was that of adding half a pound of ripe sloes to a two gallon brew. These were crushed and added just before the yeast was put in. Another was adding a little concentrated Vermouth flavouring.

All these ideas gave varied results; some people liked one while others liked another. Some people didn't like any of them, but on the whole the results were quite popular. Whatever you do, do not try out these ideas with your first efforts at beer making. Wait until you have a good deal of experience so that you are able to judge whether you would like the results of such experiments.

If you decide to add fruits to a wort ready for the yeast, do sterilize the fruit first in the following manner. This is necessary because of the yeast and bacteria on the fruit. If these are not destroyed, the chances are that they will set up undesirable ferments as they do in wines made by old-fashioned methods. Sterilizing by boiling will give the wrong kind of flavour and will produce a cloudiness difficult to remove. The simplest method is to use Campden fruit preserving tablets. See the chapter on cider making for more information about these.

Crush the fruit to be added to the wort and judge roughly how much there is and to each half-gallon (there will probably be less than this amount), add half a crushed Campden tablet dissolved in about an eggcupful of warm water. Stir this into the fruit and leave for about an hour. Then give a vigorous stirring and pour into the wort. Strain out the fruit after four or five days, and ferment on as you would if you had not used fruit at all.

I mention all these experiments to put ideas into your heads so that you will not be afraid to try almost anything once you have been making real and ordinary beers for some time.

Go ahead, experiment – it can be great fun.

Cider Making

8

Some Remarks About Cider

Like wine and beer making, cider making is on the increase to such an extent that there are now available small cider presses for home operators. Since this can be used also for crushing and pressing large amounts of fruit for making wines it would soon pay for itself. I believe one firm of home wine and home brew supplies, retails an 'assemble it yourself press' for about $7.00.

Where it is planned to make large amounts of cider a press will be an essential, but where just an occasional gallon is to be made, a press – though useful – is not essential. Most home operators 'knock up' quite a nice drop of cider without a press and do it very often, merely by making small amounts – two or three gallons frequently – instead of twenty or so. Any apples may be made into a cider of sorts, but for true cider, only true cider apples are suitable and these do not grow in all districts. And, as with wines, the quality of the cider depends on the quality of the apples used. Since weather, soil, situation, the amount of rain or sunshine during the growing and harvesting affects the quality of the apple – mainly in sugar and acid content – it follows that cider made in one year will be better than in another, depending on the weather. Skill and knowledge which can only come from experience will assist amateur cider makers to blend apples and to make allowances for deficiencies of one sort or another. But all this need not bother beginners who will not be so fastidious as to insist on the very best at the first attempt. They will know better than to expect to be able to make a cider to satisfy connoisseurs the first time and will be satisfied with jolly good second-class or 'every-day' sort of cider.

Whether cider making is going to be an attractive proposition will depend on whether cider is the favourite drink of the operator or not. There is little point in someone making cider just because this book explains how to do it unless he knows in advance that he likes cider. Not everybody does; I like it sometimes as a long refreshing drink, but I prefer a good commercial or home produced beer. In winter, I drink a lot of my own wines.

As a child I remember the travelling cider press that clanked to a standstill at the gate of my grand-father's cottage, and I can vaguely recall the urgency with which every local child was commandeered to help collect the apples. And I remember helping him with the pressing, though I cannot remember exactly how it was done. Then there was the trans-porting of the juice to the converted pig-sty he used for making the juice of the apple into the drink of the countryman. Some pretty good cider came out of that unlikely building, according to stories my late father told me – stories about men with reputations for having cast-iron intestines being flattened by just a couple of pints of 'old Dad's' concoctions.

The principle of cider making today is the same as in my grandfather's day and is, in fact, the same as it always has been. Cider making can be traced back to before the Norman conquest of this country. Before the first World War, cider was made in almost every country cottage; every farmer made it for his labourers and in almost all 'gentleman's houses' – those nearly forgotten places where the illiterate sons and daughters of the working classes were employed for a pittance, and who, incidentally, had to appear, or actually were, grateful for the opportunity – beer was made on quite a large scale.

When I was very young, one heard of the generosity of the 'gentry' who might concede to their under-paid employees drinking half a pint of the cider or beer they had spent hours of sweat-labour to produce for their master. I recall hearing of how one young lad – obviously a budding scoundrel – had drunk the accumulated drips from a barrel of beer. He was dismissed on the spot with the loss of his ten shillings – one month's wages. And according to remarks at the time, this 'young criminal' was fortunate indeed in having such a generous master, for he had lain himself open to a month in jail. But I suspect he escaped this, for the master feared he might be dubbed as mean if he had handed the lad over to the police. Such were the good old days – and like a lot of other things from the past, you can keep 'em. But not beer and cider; we'll have as much of these as we can make.

There are over twenty million gallons of cider made in factories in this country and probably as much made in odd lots by home operators every year; quite an intoxicating thought. God knows how many apples are needed for that lot!

If cider making were not worthwhile for the

amateur, production of commercial cider would double. This may be the reason for the commercial producers making such a variety of splendid ciders and advertising their goods on such a large scale – they are doubtless trying to capture the market for that other twenty million gallons. They won't do it, for not only can the amateur make a worthwhile cider, he can do it for half the price of commercially produced cider. If he grows apples, the cost is reduced by half again – he has only sugar to buy.

Those who live in cider-apple growing districts will know this well enough as those who live in cherry growing areas know well enough, so there is no point in attempting to bring the fact home to them. Those who live in such areas, would do well to find a grower and arrange for buying some of the crop annually. In some areas, growers will express the juice from an amateur cidermaker's apples for him. In others, a commercial cider producer will often sell juice expressed from the firm's cider apples to enable an amateur to make his cider with readily expressed juice.

All this being as it may it is not intended to explain how to make cider from readily expressed juice from a commercial press. Anyone with this God-sent facility at his elbow will also have neighbours with a relative working at the cider factory who will be able to tell him more about using the particular juice from the type of apple used than I could hope to. Each firm has a method to suit its particular apple, its retail trade and the people of the areas in which its products are mainly sold. And these will be a lot different to the next factory perhaps at the other end of the county or country.

My aim is to show the novice cidermaker how to use whatever types of apples are available to him. In this way he will make cider – not an imitation of some commercial product – but one peculiar to his particular needs. Furthermore, if he grows apples, he will be able to make a type or variety of cider quite unique. It will still be cider, but far and away different from the commercial product.

There is far too much of trying to ape the commercially produced these days. Wine makers, try to make wine (and do, incidentally) almost identical to commercial products. It's the same now with beer and will, I expect, be the same later on with cider. But I hope not. And I hope copying the commercial will soon die a natural death.

A number of people will ask why I have said this when obviously if we can make wines and beers as good as commercial products it is a good thing. Up to a point it is a good thing and I for one have copied commercial methods and made wines identical to world-famous commercial products. But in doing so, we forget, or just overlook the fact that in making wines from ingredients found in the field and hedgerow we are making something quite unique compared with commercial products. Our 'country wines' while still being basically country wines are now so much like commercial products that they are no longer what they used to be – country wines. They are better wines in every respect; higher in alcohol, of perfect clarity, full-bodied most of them, of good bouquet and splendid flavour. But I still feel that there is nothing to compare with the unusualness of the old country wines as I remember them as a youngster. And surely it was this unusualness that made country wines so different from the products we have turned them into. Anybody can go into the nearest pub and buy cider, but he will not be able to buy cider like the stuff he can make himself any more than a true country wine maker could buy a bottle of cowslip wine. So there it is. Copy the commercial and make something you can buy almost anywhere or stick to making something that cannot be bought anywhere or at any price.

Before making cider it should be borne in mind that to make it too strong is to make apple wine. Such would not be drinkable by the pint or half pint, but only by the wine glass. Cider is usually about 8%-9% of alcohol by volume, or around 14-15 degrees proof spirit, and this is plenty. A medium strength wine is only a little above this, so don't spoil your cider and perhaps temper by making it stronger than this.

The safest means of making sure of not making it too strong is to use a hydrometer. The use of this is explained in the beer-making section (p. 36). After the juice has been strained from the pulp, and water, if any is used, has been added, the reading is taken using the same kind of hydrometer as that used for beer making. The Specific Gravity and Alcohol Table given in the beer chapter, page 39, is quite suitable for cider. It will be seen from this that a reading of 1·070 will produce a cider of 9·2% of alcohol by volume – approximately 14° proof. This is plenty for cider. Anything stronger would be too strong. Indeed, a reading of 1·060 should be enough. If you want to make just a little drop of something stronger, take a look at the Specific Gravity and Alcohol Table in the chapter on mead making (p. 128). This covers a wider range because mead is wine, which is, naturally a stronger drink.

It is unlikely that apple juice will contain enough sugar to make the amount of alcohol required, therefore, some will have to be added. Now, suppose you take the reading of the juice and it registers 1·040. You decide you want more alcohol than this figure will give you; all you have to do is to add sugar to give the reading you want which in turn will give the amount of alcohol you require. This will be readily seen by consulting the table already mentioned. Let us suppose you want to raise the gravity by twenty degrees on the hydrometer, all you have to do is to bear in mind that 2¼ ounces of sugar will raise the gravity of a gallon of juice by five degrees, 5 ounces being needed for 2 gallons, 10 ounces for 4 gallons and so on. Therefore, if you want to raise the gravity by twenty degrees in one gallon, you merely calculate thus: 2¼ ounces of sugar will raise it by five degrees, so to raise it by twenty, you must add four times 2¼ ounces – 9 ounces per gallon.

It will be seen then that a cider of any strength may be made merely by increasing the amount of sugar. But as already explained, over-strong ciders should not be the aim of anybody simply because, like beers, cider is for drinking in larger quantities than wines.

Dry Cider

This is the easiest to make because if just enough sugar is added to make the amount of alcohol required, the cider will turn out dry when all the sugar has been used up in producing the necessary alcohol. Therefore, all you need do is to allow fermentation to go on until it ceases and the cider becomes clear. It may then be siphoned off the deposit into bottles or into jars and used as draught cider.

Medium Dry, Medium Sweet or Sweet Cider

These are not really any more difficult to make than dry cider, but it must be borne in mind that to add more sugar at the outset in the hope of leaving some unfermented to sweeten the cider will only result in this extra sugar being converted to alcohol so that the cider becomes a high alcohol dry cider or rather dry apple wine.

As will be seen by those who have read the chapter on mead making (p. 124), up to two and a half pounds of sugar per gallon will be fermented out by the yeast – and this amount will produce 14% of alcohol by volume; much too much for cider. Therefore, the only way to make a medium dry, medium sweet or sweet cider is to add just enough sugar to give the alcohol required and to finish with a dry cider and then sweeten it to taste. But because this sweetening will give rise to further fermentation, we must preserve the cider, or in other words, we must destroy the yeast so that further fermentation cannot take place.

Using Campden fruit preserving tablets for this is the easiest way out of the problem. Having made the dry cider with the amount of alcohol required – this will result automatically when the right amount of sugar has been used – so much in the juice and so much added – the amount of cider must be measured after sweetening to taste. To each gallon, crush and dissolve two Campden tablets in a little warmed cider and then stir this into the bulk. Bung down and keep in a cool place. This should be enough to prevent further fermentation, but if after a week or two, the bung blows out of the jar, similar treatment with a further tablet per gallon will be necessary. Keeping in a cool place is a great help in preventing further fermentation. This is because yeast likes warmth – indeed, it must have warmth to ferment well. But a cool atmosphere, the amount of alcohol present in the cider, together with the preserving qualities of the Campden tablets is usually sufficient to prevent further yeast growth.

Sparkling Cider

Not quite so easy to make as other sorts; the difference being the same as making draught and gaseous beers. In making sparkling cider one must make a dry cider first and then prime this with sugar as directed under Priming (p. 58). The bottles for sparkling cider must be the strong screw-stoppered sort. If these are used, the draught, dry cider may be made into sparkling cider quite readily. But as most people want their cider crystal-clear the problem of removing the inevitable yeast deposit that will form in each bottle after priming will arise. As in beer making, if a good sedimentary yeast is used, this will stick to the bottom of the bottles so that all but a little of the cider may be poured off clear. I do not know who first said this, but he was absolutely right when saying: 'The English drink with their eyes rather than their palate; they will drink anything provided it is crystal clear.' How true, and how much time and trouble they would save themselves if they were content to drink ciders and other alcoholic drinks with just a haze in them. They will drink fruit juices as cloudy as a muddy puddle, but just because it has been seen to be crystal clear, it now seems that wines, cider, and the pale-coloured beers must also be crystal clear. The faint yeast haze found in these drinks sometimes does not mar the flavour, only the appearance. If you cannot tolerate the idea of a yeast deposit in your bottles of cider, you may remove it, but this is not as easy as it sounds; though after some experience it can be done quite effectively.

The primed cider is put into bottles, the stoppers are screwed home and the bottles stood in a cardboard crate upside down. This allows for the yeast to settle on the stoppers of the bottles. A gentle twist from day to day will assist the yeast to slide down the necks so that when the renewed fermentation has ceased after about a week – longer in some cases – all the yeast has settled to about a quarter-inch-thick deposit on the stoppers. The bottles are then held upside down over the sink, the stopper of each is given a twist in the open direction and then back again at once. This action allows the gas to squirt out the deposit. You won't do it first time, but if you are patient, you will learn to do it with practice.

Freezing is another method, but few have the facility, so there is little point in including details here.

9

Making Cider

Ingredients

One variety of apple alone will not make for a balanced cider. The chances are that it will lack flavour, body, and in fact, most of the characteristics of a good cider. Almost any sort of garden apple may be used but do use some sweet, a few sharp and, if possible a few dry sorts of apple, or some pears not over-loaded with juice. It would not be sensible to recommend any particular blend of apples simply because one will have to use those available; only those living in cider-growing areas will have the true cider apple at his disposal and he will already have someone at his elbow to tell him how best to handle them.

To select the right type of apple for the job would involve knowledge of the acid, sugar and tannin content of each variety, and hardly any amateur is likely to have such knowledge at his disposal. If he had, he would not necessarily know how to utilize it.

So, at first attempt, chances will have to be taken on just how the final cider comes up to hopes and expectations. But with a little experience gained in making a few lots, any operator should be able to learn how to blend the apples he has available in order to make the cider he is after. Alternatively, he can make several different sorts in small quantities and then blend them to get an improved produce as wine makers blend their elderberry, damson and plum wines. You would be surprised (if you are not already a wine maker), just how this making of small lots of varied, yet similar wines and then blending them makes for some really top-class products. This does not mean that the individual wines are not in themselves top-class products. It is merely that in a poor season one of these wines might disappoint. It is at times like this when blending with other wines will make that disappointing wine into something quite remarkable.

And so it is with ciders. Small lots may be improved by blending with each other, but a large amount of one sort if it is not up to expectations has to be drunk as it is. So use of your common sense will bring you very close indeed to making the cider you like at first attempt – even if it does mean blending two or three lots made with different sorts of different mixtures of varieties of apples.

Sugar

White household sugar is quite suitable, but very good results are obtained when golden syrup is used. Try this, for many people find this gives some character and flavour to a cider made from unsuitable apples. Demerara sugar should not be used; nor should other brown sugars. Either white sugar, which adds nothing but sweetness, or golden syrup, which adds both colour and some little flavour, are the best to use.

If golden syrup is used, more will have to be used

to raise the gravity to the required level. Stir in a little at a time, taking the readings after each addition until the required reading is obtained. Pound for pound, there is less sugar in syrup than in dry sugar itself, this is the reason for using more syrup than sugar.

Water

Many people find sugar additions difficult, or they fear that adding water will reduce the flavour of the cider. They therefore overheat the juice to dissolve the sugar, and thus dissolve or make active pectin in the apple, and as every wine maker knows pectin causes cloudiness difficult to remove. So let me make it clear that the use of a little water will not reduce to any appreciable extent the flavour of the cider – provided the amount used is the absolute minimum needed to dissolve the sugar, this being about one pint to two pounds of sugar.

Put the sugar in the water and bring slowly to the boil, stirring frequently to avoid sticking to the bottom of the saucepan or burning. When sugar is dissolved, cool the resulting syrup and then stir into the apple juice. The procedure after this is the same as already stated.

Method

The apples should be washed in water, and even if a press is available, they will first have to be pulp. This is best done if they are put in an open tub and pounded with the end of a stout pole. Mincing small quantities is a good means of extracting the juice. Large quantities are a problem, but if you know a friendly butcher, he might be willing to mince them for you with his much larger machine.

Modern domestic fruit juice machines are ideal for small amounts of ordinary fruit, but are not suitable for apples or pears. One can overcome to some extent the problem of pressing to get the maximum juice by fermenting the pulp-pounded apple. This method of making cider is described separately.

When using a press, put in only small amounts of pounded apple at a time otherwise you'll not be able to screw down properly. Directions are supplied with the different presses and because each is used in a slightly different way and the directions will vary with each press; for this reason I cannot give here general purpose instructions to cover each one. Minced apple may be strained through a strong coarse cloth and wrung out, that is, when all juice that will drip out has done so, two people may twist the cloth in opposite directions while the part containing the pulp is held over the vessel catching the juice.

Having produced all the juice you can, strain a sample as free as possible of particles of apple pulp and take the reading using a specific gravity hydrometer reading from 1·000 to 1·100 – the same as that used for home brewing. From this reading you will be able to see how much sugar the juice contains and calculate how much to add to raise the gravity to give the amount of alcohol you want to make.

Having done this, the sugar is added (or syrup if this is being used). Dry sugar will have to be dissolved in a little of the juice warmed until the sugar is dissolved. Do not make juice hot otherwise a clearing problem may crop up later on.

Where only a gallon or so is being made and therefore comparatively little sugar being added, this may be dissolved in a little hot water – say half a pint and then added to the juice. This half pint is not likely to reduce the flavour of the juice to any great extent, but because it will reduce slightly the hydrometer reading, another ounce per gallon of juice should be added.

The type of vessel used for fermentation purposes will depend on the amount of cider being made. If ten or so gallons are being made an open barrel will be needed. But if it's just a gallon or two a two-gallon polythene pail will be ideal – these hold a little over two gallons.

Having produced the juice and added the sugar, the amount you have should be assessed as accurately as possible or measured, for it is at this stage where we must destroy the yeast and bacteria in the juice.*

To each gallon crush and dissolve one Campden fruit preserving tablet. Dissolve this in about an egg-cupful of warm water and stir into the bulk. Leave for a few hours, stir vigorously and then add your yeast. This adding of Campden tablets may be carried out before adding the sugar if you wish.

It is now time to add the yeast. A good all-purpose wine yeast is quite suitable, but when these are used, fermentation is rather slower than when one of the vigorous yeasts in granulated form is used. The granulated yeasts do not settle and stick hard to the bottom of bottles as wine yeasts do. But this is not important where a draught cider is being made. Dried wine yeast in tablet form may be started off as a nucleus as directed for reclaiming yeasts from

* For causes of spoilage see p. 115.

commercial beers. The tablet is put into a small amount of water in which some sugar has been dissolved by boiling. When cool, the tablet is put in; in a few days the yeast will be fermenting. This should be prepared three or four days in advance of preparing the juice. Dried yeast in granulated form may be added as it is, as this usually starts fermenting within a few hours, whereas wine yeasts take several days to get going, and it is important not to leave the juice inactive for this period. Fermentation will be seen as frothing on the surface. After about ten days, the cider is transferred to gallon or two-gallon jars – according to the amount being made. Fermentation locks are then fitted. The use of these is included in the chapter on beer making (p. 35). An illustration is on page 154.

When the lock has been fitted the cider is kept in a warm place until all fermentation has ceased.

This will be draught cider of an alcoholic content according to the amount of sugar used. It will also be dry.

Sweetening this or making it into a sparkling cider has been described at the end of the previous chapter.

Cider does not improve greatly on keeping. But it should be kept for three months at least. After six months there is never an improvement.

Cider from Apple Pulp

Where there is no means of separating the juice from the pulp, it will be found that quite good cider may be made from fermenting the pulp. There will be some loss of juice if this is done because some will inevitably be left in the pulp.

The process is simplicity itself. One merely proceeds to produce the pulp as directed above, and instead of pressing out the juice, the whole lot is fermented. Sugar is dissolved in as little water as possible. This is boiled together and added to the pulp. The pulp is then measured and treated with Campden tablets as already directed. The yeast is then added and fermentation allowed to proceed for seven-eight days. After this, the cider is strained free of apple particles. The pulp should be allowed to drain. While this is draining, a sheet of polythene should be spread over the surface of the pulp and down round the sides of the vessel receiving the drippings. This should be tied in place with thin string or kept in place with strong elastic to prevent airborne diseases reaching it. Leave for two or three hours. Then put the strained cider into jars and fit fermentation lock. Do not squeeze the pulp too much.

Causes of Spoilage

Readers of my wine books will know all about these, but I must include details here for the benefit of those not in possession of either of them.

On the skins of apples there are various strains of yeast and some bacteria. These get into the juice when it is in the process of being pressed from the apples. These yeasts and bacteria can start souring ferments and turn the alcohol into acetic acid – vinegar. Boiling the juice will produce a cider that will never clear – though it will destroy the troublesome yeast and bacteria. Therefore, we must destroy the yeast and bacteria without boiling. Here again, Campden fruit-preserving tablets do the job for us.

Having expressed the juice, one Campden tablet per gallon is crushed and dissolved in a little warm water and stirred into the juice. Two may be used to make sure there will be no souring ferments, but if two are used, the juice should be stirred vigorously after one hour and then again after ten minutes. This will liberate much of the gas so that the yeast added to ferment the juice is not also killed as it is put in.

The gas produced by the Campden tablets is known as sulphur-dioxide or $S.O_2$. This method of destroying unwanted yeast and bacteria is used extensively by both commercial and amateur wine makers.

All bottles and stoppers must be washed in a solution of sulphur dioxide made up by dissolving 2 oz. sodium metabisulphite in half a gallon of warm water. Half a pint of this is poured into the first bottle, then into the next and next and so on. When a dozen have been done this half pint is discarded. The bottles are then rinsed with boiled water that has cooled; they are then ready to receive the cider. Jars for draught cider are treated in the same fashion. The bulk of the sterilizing solution may be kept for further use. Best to use a glass-stoppered or rubber-stoppered bottle for this. Plenty of chemists will let you have one for about a shilling.

Acidity in Finished Cider

The most common fault in an amateur's cider is acidity. This is because most apples contain more acid than is needed for pleasant cider. Diluting the juice to lessen the acidity before fermentation usually results in a poorly-flavoured cider. Balancing the acidity using acidemetric apparatus, is almost certainly beyond the scope of beginners because not only is expensive apparatus needed, but also some laboratory experience.

However, if a cider turns out too acid, some of the acid may be removed quite simply by anyone. The only risk is that of removing too much. Even this can be rectified, but this involves adding more acid. Better to proceed with caution and to get the less-acid cider you are after at first or second attempt. Now let us suppose a cider is only a little too acid. Removing a little acid is quite simple. Take a quart of the cider (a quart of each gallon); take a little of this quart and dissolve in this by stirring about a quarter ounce of precipitated chalk – from any chemist for a few coppers. When dissolved, stir this into the quart. Leave until the sample is clear again and then siphon the clear cider off the chalk deposit. Having done this, return the treated cider to the bulk. The acid will have been removed from the quart by the chalk, and this completely acid-free cider going into the bulk should be enough to reduce the acidity of the rest of it. If it is found that not enough acid has been removed, repeat the process, but with less chalk this time. If by accident, too much acid is removed so that you have a flat almost insipid cider, the remedy is to add either citric acid from a chemist or lemon juice.

MAKING PERRY

Whereas cider may be still (draught) or sparkling, true perry is a sparkling drink – that is, it is not made as a still or draught perry, though I can think of no reason for not making it as still perry if this suits the individual operator. The fact that it is 'still' will mean that, strictly speaking, it will not be perry because it is not sparkling; after all, champagne would not be champagne without its sparkle. Nevertheless, those with an abundance of pears should try their hand at making perry either sparkling or still – as it suits them. But do take note of all I have had to say about sparkling cider in the chapter on cider making.

Perry may be made in exactly the same way as cider. Dessert pears are not needed. A mixture of pears; some sweet, some lacking juice and on the dry side, some cooking pears and in fact some of those little hard ones that children love to get their teeth into may all go in together. But where only one variety is available, a few from an outside source should be obtained and added, otherwise the perry will lack character. Where additional pears are not obtainable, a few crab-apples will do nicely—say one pound to every ten pounds of pears.

A dry sparkling or merely a dry still pear wine or perry low in alcohol – say 8-9% by volume is a nice drink. See p. 39 for relation between sugar content and alcohol.

Pears usually contain enough tannin, therefore none need be added – so put the tea-pot away. Acid will be needed; this should be added at the rate of a quarter ounce to the gallon of juice obtained. Where some water has been used to make a bit more of the juice, a little more acid should be added because in diluting the juice you will reduce the acid content.

Mead Making

10

An Introduction

As I have written elsewhere, mead is one of the oldest alcoholic drinks known to man.

In the early days wild bees were the only source of honey and with this honey some sort of crude mead was made. Today with bee-keeping on the increase and with the commercial production of honey it is only natural that mead making should also increase.

Mead may be bought from any wine merchant, the price ranging from about eight to twelve shillings a bottle. These are, as one would expect, the very finest meads. But it does not mean that you would like them. You will probably prefer your own once you get used to making it. As one who makes enormous quantities of all kinds of wines, I can assure you that I prefer my own to commercial products – except for the very finest sherries which amateurs cannot successfully imitate.

The honey for mead making is best obtained direct from a bee-keeper in the area in which you live, and you will be surprised how many there are when you begin to make enquiries. Solidified honey is not suitable as this is usually adulterated with invert sugar. By this I do not mean harmed in any way, but in this solidified honey there is less pure honey than in the familiar syrup or comb honeys.

Buy in bulk of at least seven pounds and save a lot of money. Do not buy from shops who only retail in half-pound pots; if you do, your mead will cost a fortune. By buying direct, either from a bee-keeper or from one of the home brewing and home wine supply firms listed at the end of this book, your meads need cost you no more than two shillings a bottle.

There are strong and mild flavoured honeys and dark and light coloured. Only you can decide which to use for your special purpose. All are suitable for an initial experiment. If after your first attempt you feel that perhaps a milder-flavoured honey would have given better results you will know what to do next time. Or it may be that a stronger-flavoured honey should have been used. Either way, your first attempt will be well worth drinking. I make these points merely to show that with a variety of honeys available, you might not hit the nail on the head first time. It will be a case of you thinking: now, I like this, but if I had used . . . I'm sure it would be even better.

And from there you begin to experiment in small amounts using different types of honey.

Types of Mead

As with all wines, mead may be sweet, medium or dry. It may also be sparkling. To make sparkling mead one must start with a gravity of 1·100 and when fermentation has finished the hydrometer reading should be 1·000 or less. The mead may then be primed as for beers, and put in screw-stoppered bottles where refermentation will charge the mead with gas in the same way as beers. But because we use rather more sugar in mead making (the sugar being in the honey), it is not always safe to rely on the hydrometer to give deadly accurate results of fermentation. By this, I mean that we are sometimes unsure whether *all* sugar has been fermented out. Now, if we primed a mead to make it sparkling and some sugar remained unfermented, this, in addition to that used from priming, would charge the mead with so much gas that the bottles might explode. So, my advice is to leave sparkling meads to those with experience, unless you are certain that all sugar has been fermented out before priming.

There are many sorts of mead: Sack mead is sweet mead of about 14% of alcohol by volume; Metheglin is the same as Sack mead but is spiced according to whim – and often ruined, incidentally, by the over zealous. This may be dry or sweet.

The spices and other flavouring are for some reason referred to as cruits. Their variety is limited only by the scope of the imagination. I am not fond of spiced mead – at least, not that flavoured with ginger and clove. Not only do I dislike it for itself, but I consider it a waste of good honey to use ginger and cloves. If you want a ginger-flavoured or clove-flavoured wine, surely less regal basic ingredients could be used. Many people ruin elderberry wine with cloves so that they have clove wine rather than an elderberry wine finely flavoured with clove. So don't spoil good spiced meads or Metheglins by overspicing.

Rosemary, cloves, nutmeg, ginger, mace and cinnamon are the usual flavourings and these must be added to suit the tastes of the operator. Start with a little and increase the amount until you have the strength of flavour required. This will vary greatly with each operator and the only guidance I can give is not to add more than one clove to the gallon to start with and only a very small amount of bruised root ginger. Better not to add enough and be able to increase the amount in safety than to over-do it at the start.

Alcohol Content of Mead

Unlike beers and cider, meads, being wines, are drunk in small quantities. Therefore, we make them as strong as we can. The amount of alcohol we can make in meads is limited by the capacity of the yeast we add to withstand alcohol. And here it is important to understand that yeast cannot live in a solution containing more than 14% of alcohol by volume. This is the usual amount that will destroy the yeast. But under certain circumstances, and with suitable yeast the percentage might be as high as eighteen. On the whole an amateur is unlikely to produce more than 16%; this is because he is unlikely to be able to carry out his ferments under laboratory conditions with constantly favourable temperatures and a scientifically balanced must.

Therefore, it is always wise to presume that you will not make more than 14% by volume and work accordingly.

Now, honey is made up of approximately 70% sugar; the remainder is made up of some impurities – such as yeast and bacteria, water, albumen and ash. Our concern is the amount of sugar, for it is upon this that the amount of alcohol we make depends. The yeast and bacteria are also our concern, but these are dealt with under the Causes of Spoilage – page 133.

Recipes for mead follow, but here it is as well to point out that if you want to be sure of the amount of alcohol you make, then the same type of hydrometer as used for beer brewing becomes essential.

In the ordinary way, three to four pounds of honey are used to make one gallon of mead. And because the amount of sugar will vary slightly in the various honeys available, there is no guarantee when using recipes that the mead will turn out to precisely the fine degree of sweetness or dryness required. Use little honey and the wine will be dry, of course; use a lot of honey and the wine will be sweet. Whether too dry or too sweet or merely medium dry-sweet will depend on the amount of sugar the honey contains.

As will be seen in the recipes the honey is mixed with water, and in the ordinary way, no sugar is added because the honey contains enough.

If recipes are being followed, and if readers are satisfied with the results of using them, as most will be, then all well and good. But those who want to make their meads to fine degrees of sweetness or dryness will have to use the hydrometer, and in so doing, these operators will be able to calculate at the start, how much alcohol they will make in addition to knowing whether their mead will be dry, medium-dry, medium-sweet or sweet. The only way to do this is to mix the honey with water as given in a recipe using the smallest amount given. A sample is then put into the hydrometer sample flask and the hydrometer itself slipped into this. The flask is stood on a level surface and the reading taken where the sample cuts across the stem. This reading is compared with the Hydrometer and Alcohol Table for Meads on page 128. Let us say that the reading is 1·090. As will be seen from the table, this will make 11·9% of alcohol by volume, and the mead will be bone dry. Now, we can add more honey – or if this is in short supply, sugar – to increase the gravity to 1·100. If this is done, 13·4% of alcohol will be made, but the mead will still be dry. Not until you go above the figure of 1·110 will the mead begin to turn out sweet. This is because two and a half pounds of sugar will be used up in making 14·5% of alcohol by volume and this amount of sugar per gallon is represented by the reading of 1·100. Actually the exact amount of sugar for a reading of 1·110 is an unimportant fraction above two and a half pounds. Therefore, if a bone dry mead is required you should start off with a reading of 1·100 or 1·110 and end up with a dry mead of between 13·4% and 14·5% of alcohol by volume. Because this figure of 1·110 represents the maximum amount of sugar the yeast can use, it follows that if a higher gravity is used to start with (in other words, if more honey is used or sugar added), all sugar or honey in excess of 1·110 on the hydrometer, will be left unfermented to sweeten the mead. A reading of 1·120 will make mead just a little above dryness or medium-dry, while ten degrees above this will make for medium sweet and so on until sweet mead results. Now take a look at the table on page 128 and you will see just how all this works out in practice.

It may be that your first reading will be below the first figure on the table – this being 1·070. Do not let this confuse you, merely add sugar or honey until the reading you want is reached. On the other hand, it could be that the first reading quite by chance is above 1·100. In this case, if a bone-dry mead is wanted, a little more water will reduce the gravity reading, to the required 1·100.

Bear in mind that if one gallon has a reading of 1·100, two gallons with the same amount of honey in each will have the same reading. Three gallons with the same amount of honey in each will also have the same reading. It will be seen from this that no matter how much mead is being made the reading will be the same as if one gallon is being made. This is because each gallon contains the same amount of honey. For example, let us suppose three and a half pounds of honey made up to one gallon gives a reading of 1·100; seven pounds made up to two gallons will still give a reading of 1·100. Similarly, ten and a half pounds made up to three gallons will also give this reading, and so on up the scale no matter how much mead is being made.

Important. If you start with a gravity of 1·100 to make a dry mead – the most popular sort – and this turns out medium sweet or sweet, then it means that fermentation has stuck, in other words, it has stopped prematurely. See STICKING FERMENTS page 132.

If it had not stuck, fermentation would have gone on to make the amount of alcohol required so that all the sugar in the honey had been fermented out, leaving a dry mead.

Hydrometer and Alcohol Table for Meads

Specific Gravity (hydrometer reading)	*Potential Alcohol by Volume*	*Degrees proof (Approx.)*	*Type of Mead*
1·070	9·0%	15·6	dry
1·080	10·5%	17·8	dry
1·090	11·9%	20·0	dry
1·100	13·4%	22·9	dry
1·110	14·5%	25·2	dry
1·120	14·5%		medium-dry
1·130	14·5%		medium-sweet
1·140	14·5%		sweet

Those using the hydrometer may take the reading when all fermentation has ceased to check the amount of alcohol made. Those starting off with a gravity of 1·110 or below should end with a reading of 1·000 or less. Those beginning with a reading above 1·110, will find that the figure above this will still register on the hydrometer. For example, if they began with a reading of 1·120, they should end up with a reading of 1·010. This is because sugar representing 110 degrees on the hydrometer has been fermented out. In this case, the resulting mead is of 14·5% of alcohol by volume with sugar representing 10 degrees on the hydrometer left unfermented to sweeten the mead slightly. The same will apply to all readings above the 1·110 figure

Note. Many people are puzzled when diluting honey after taking the reading with a hydrometer. One person wrote that they had a mixture of honey and water with a specific gravity of 1·180. He wanted to reduce this to make two gallons with a reading of 1·090. In other words he wanted a bone-dry mead of 11·9% of alcohol by volume. But, he wrote, 'surely in making this up to two gallons I shall reduce the reading to ·590?' The point overlooked here, of course, was that the water he would have added already has the gravity of 1·000. Therefore, no matter how much water he added, the reading would not go below 1·000. He had overlooked that the figures above the 1·000 mark are all we are concerned with as it is these that record the amount of sugar in the mixture. In his case, if he had done as he wanted to he would have done the right thing, for he would have reduced the reading of ·180 – the reading above the 1·000 which represented the sugar content of his mixture – to the figure ·090. The fact that his hydrometer would record a reading of 1·090 is because the water in the mixture has the gravity of 1·000. To make it even more simple, look at it this way –

Water – 1·000
Sugar 90

S.G. – 1.090 or total gravity of mixture.

Certain operators using the hydrometer, like to use enough honey to give a reading of 1·100 and to ferment this, as they know that this is the best figure to start with. I do recommend this for it will be found that whichever yeast is used, it will ferment much better when not too much sugar is present. The reading of 1·100 is the best to use as this ensures that the yeast action is not impeded and that maximum alcohol will be obtained. This means, of course, that unless more honey or sugar is added, the mead will be dry. But because the yeast does better when less sugar is present, more sugar or honey may be added after some of the sugar already there has been used up.

Therefore, always start off with a gravity of 1·100 and add sugar or honey representing the figure above this after say five or six days fermentation. Sugar is best for this later addition as it is easier to calculate how much to use. $2\frac{1}{4}$ oz. will raise the gravity of one gallon by five degrees; 5 oz. will raise it ten degrees. Therefore, if you want to start with a gravity of 1·110, start, actually, with a reading of 1·100 and add five ounces of sugar later on. Ten ounces added after starting with a gravity of 1·100 will have the effect of having started with a reading of 1·120. These points are made for those who will want to make less dry or sweet meads.

FERMENTATION

Yeast for Mead Making

Anybody can use baker's yeast and get a mead of sorts with possibly a yeast haze in it and a bakehouse mustiness into the bargain. It is well worth while getting a good yeast either dried or in liquid form. Dried all-purpose wine yeast does an excellent job here, but those with a good deal of experience in making a variety of top-class meads insist on a certain variety of yeast. Madeira yeast is fancied by some while others swear by Tokay yeast. Sherry and Maurey yeasts are also popular. So do not use baker's yeast, unless you want an inferior product, which, of course, amounts to a waste of honey – and money.

Aids to Good Fermentation

As with all alcoholic products a good fermentation from the outset to the end is important for good results. Now, in itself, and because honey is mostly sugar and water, it is not the best medium for good fermentation. This is because unlike fruit juices it contains no acid or tannin – both of which are essentials to good fermentation. As will be seen in the recipes we add acid either as citric acid easily obtained quite cheaply from any chemist or the same stuff in the form of lemon juice. Tannin is added in the form of tea; tea being a useful and cheap source of tannin. These two constituents are also important to the flavour of the finished product. Without them the mead would appear lifeless; in other words it would lack character, bite – or even 'guts' if you like to put it that way. Also lacking in honey are essential elements found in most fruit juices. This deficiency is easily made up by adding nutrient salts in tablet form. These are known as yeast nutrients and are obtainable from dealers in home wine and home brewing equipment. When to add the tablet is given in the recipes. Temperature is also an important consideration.

Yeast, as we have seen in other parts of this book, must have warmth if it is to reproduce itself. And as already explained, it is this reproduction going on that uses up the sugar and produces alcohol. The ideal temperature is between 65°-70°f. It is not always possible to maintain this, but where it *is* possible, it certainly should be maintained. Failing this, a warm place where the temperature remains fairly constant will do. But on no account allow the mead-in-making to become too warm, otherwise fermentation might stop prematurely or 'stick'.

Sticking Ferments

When fermentation stops before the maximum alcohol the yeast can make is actually made, we say that fermentation has stuck. The main cause of this is too high or too low a temperature. Also, lack of acid or tannin or both. Now, provided the recipes are followed, and the fermenting mead kept warm, fermentation should not 'stick', but sometimes it does. Where it sticks when only about 2% below the maximum alcohol, nothing much is lost. In fact, you might waste a lot of time in trying to get fermentation on the go again. 2% is not important, so if you obviously have a good mead with near enough the alcohol content you aimed at, be satisfied rather than try to make it better. But where a dry mead was aimed at, a dry mead should result. This is because not enough sugar was in the original must to slow up fermentation. And since dry mead is preferred in this case, fermentation must be induced to recommence.

To define the reason for a ferment having 'stuck' is difficult for beginners – especially when they have added tannin and acid and kept their musts warm. But here is the usual cause, over-warmth or not warm enough. Where it is clear that a must has become too warm, allow it to become quite cold and then warm it again gradually, but be careful this time not to let it become over-heated. Where it has become cold, gradual warming by keeping in a warm place will usually get fermentation on the go again. On no account, attempt to heat the must quickly. If these two remedies fail after a few days of trial, the need for a tiny additional amount of tannin or acid may be indicated, and this should be tried. Just a few drops of strong, freshly-made tea or a few – three or four – crystals of citric acid should be added. Where crystals are not available, a few drops of lemon juice should be tried. If all this fails, then it could be that all nutrient matter has been used up and a further half to whole nutrient tablet should be crushed and added. After each of the recommended additions, give the must three or four days before adding anything else. It often needs this period of time to get a sticking ferment on the go again. For example, if you try extra acid, wait three or four days to see if fermentation gets going again, if it does not, then try something else I have recommended.

Use of Fermentation Lock

The use of the fermentation lock has already been described in the brewing and cider-making chapters. Here it is necessary only to say that we use it in mead making to ensure maximum alcohol is made and to prevent airborne diseases reaching the must. Follow directions already given in the chapters mentioned above and fit the lock at the time given in the recipes. *See illustrations of the fermentation lock on pages* 154 *and* 155.

Causes of Spoilage

As already mentioned (p. 125), honey contains bacteria and yeasts. These, like the yeasts and bacteria on the skins of fruit, are the main causes of spoilage. The method we shall use, ensures that they are destroyed; I mention them because too many people are still trying to make mead without sterilizing the honey-water mixture before they begin. If not sterilized, these yeasts and bacteria will almost certainly start spoiling ferments to produce souring, bitterness or vinegar flavours. In its undiluted state, the concentration of sugar prevents their action, but as soon as this is reduced by diluting with water, they are ready to spring into action and spoil the mead. Where small amounts of mead are being made – say one or two gallons at a time – boiling the mixture is the easiest means of sterilizing. But where larger amounts are being made, a large enough vessel for boiling might be hard to come by; in this case, the mixture may be sterilized by adding two Campden tablets per gallon. These are crushed and dissolved in a little warm water and stirred into the mixture. This is left for a few hours and then given a brisk stirring before the yeast is added. But as most beginners will be making one or two gallon lots to start with they will do the heat sterilization method as given in the recipes.

11

Recipes for Mead

Boiling one gallon of honey and water mixture often proves difficult owing to a vessel holding a good deal more than a gallon being required. Therefore, I have arranged the method to allow for half the water to be used at the start – or approximately half, it will not matter if you are a pint over or under the amount given to start with. As will be seen, the mixture is made up to one gallon before the yeast is added, and this is all that matters.

Dry Table Mead

3½ lb. honey · ¼ oz. citric acid
¼ pint strong freshly-made tea
yeast · nutrient

Mix honey with about half gallon of hot water, bring slowly to boil and boil for two minutes. Turn into polythene pail, add citric acid and tea and make up to one gallon with boiling water. Allow to cool to approximately 65°f. and then add yeast and nutrient. Cover as directed for beers (p. 51) and ferment in warm place for ten-fourteen days.

If using hydrometer, take reading when mixture has cooled to the point where the yeast is added.

After ten-fourteen days, pour into gallon jar,

leaving as much deposit behind as you can. Fit fermentation lock and leave in warm place until all fermentation has ceased. It may be several months before this happens, but when fermentation has ceased and the mead is clear, it should be siphoned off the deposit into another jar and bunged down and kept for one year or it may be bottled and sealed; then some may be used right away and a few bottles kept to mature. Don't judge young mead for it is not at its best; at a year old it will have mellowed and developed its full flavour and bouquet.

Medium-Sweet Mead

4-4½ lb. honey · ¼ oz. citric acid
¼ pint strong freshly-made tea
yeast · nutrient

Mix honey with about half a gallon of hot water, bring slowly to boil and boil for two minutes. Turn into polythene pail, add citric acid and tea and make up to one gallon with boiling water. Allow to cool to approximately 65°f., then add yeast and nutrient. Cover as directed for beers (p. 51) and ferment in warm place for ten-fourteen days. After this, proceed as for DRY TABLE MEAD on page 135.

Sweet Mead

4½-5 lb. honey · ¼ oz. citric acid
¼ pint strong freshly-made tea
yeast · nutrient

Mix honey with about half gallon of hot water,

bring slowly to boil and boil for two minutes. Turn into polythene pail, add citric acid and tea and make up to one gallon with boiling water. Allow to cool to approximately 65°f., then add yeast and nutrient. Cover as directed for beers (p. 51) and ferment in warm place for ten-fourteen days.

After this, proceed as for DRY TABLE MEAD on page 135.

FLOWER-FLAVOURED MEADS

These meads flavoured with flowers are something quite special. The flavour of the flowers in these is not so marked as when more flowers are used to make flower wines. The amounts of flowers given in these recipes give a delightful background flavour while allowing the flavour of the honey to remain unmasked. These 'meads' are not, strictly speaking, meads, but I call them meads because the basic material is honey. All flower mead recipes make for medium sweet wines. Those who know in advance that they must have all wines dry should use not more than three-and-a-half pounds of honey instead of the four pounds given in the recipes. Those who must have all wines on the sweet side should use not less than four-and-a-half pounds and not more than five pounds instead of the four pounds given in the recipes.

Clover Mead

Use purple (sometimes called mauve) clover.

4 lb. honey · ¼ oz. citric acid
¼ pint strong freshly-made tea
2-3 pints clover head · yeast · nutrient

The clover heads should be loosely packed in the measure and not pressed down hard.

Mix honey with about half a gallon of hot water, bring slowly to boil and boil for two minutes.

Turn into polythene pail containing the clover heads. Add citric acid and tea and make up to one gallon with boiling water. Add extra quart of boiling water to make up for the space occupied by the flower heads – regardless of the number of pints used.

Allow to cool to approximately 65°f. and add yeast and nutrient. Cover as directed for beers (p. 51) and ferment in warm place for five-six days.

Strain out flower heads and return strained liquor to fermenting vessel. Cover again as before and continue to ferment thus for a further five-six days. Then siphon into gallon jar, leaving as much deposit behind as you can. Fit fermentation lock and leave until all fermentation has ceased. Fermentation may go on for as long as several months. When finished and the wine is clear it should be siphoned into another jar and bunged down for one year, after which it may be bottled.

Rose Petal Mead

4 lb. honey · ¼ oz. citric acid
¼ pint strong freshly-made tea
3 pints rose petals · yeast · nutrient

Rose petals should be loosely packed in the measure and not pressed down.

Mix honey with about half-gallon hot water, bring slowly to boil and boil for two minutes. Turn into polythene pail containing rose petals, add citric acid and tea and make up to one gallon with boiling water. Add extra *1 pint* of boiling water to make up for the petals' space. Allow mixture to cool to approximately 65°f. and add yeast and nutrient.

Cover as for beers and ferment in warm place for five-six days. Strain out petals, return strained liquor to fermenting vessel, cover as before and leave thus to ferment for a further five-six days.

Thereafter proceed as for CLOVER MEAD on page 137.

Gorse Mead

A beautiful pale gold wine.

4 lb. honey · ¼ oz. citric acid
¼ pint strong freshly-made tea
3 pints gorse flowers · yeast · nutrient

Mix honey with about half a gallon of hot water, bring slowly to the boil and boil for two minutes. Turn into polythene pail containing gorse flowers. Add citric acid and tea and make up to one gallon with boiling water. Add extra *1 pint* to make up for space occupied by flowers. Allow mixture to cool to approximately 65°f. and add yeast and nutrient.

Note. Flowers should be loosely packed in the measure and not packed down hard.

Thereafter proceed as for CLOVER MEAD on page 137.

Dandelion Mead

4 lb. honey · ¼ oz. citric acid
¼ pint strong freshly-made tea
2-3 pints dandelion petals · yeast · nutrient

Dandelions should be gathered on a dry sunny day. Petals only should be used, so hold the green calyx in one hand and the petals in another and pull apart. If this is done a few hours after the flowers have been gathered the heads will have closed up making this job very easy. Be careful not to allow the tiniest part of any stem get into the mixture otherwise the bitterness of dandelion 'milk' will get into the wine. Loosely pack petals in measure – do not pack down hard.

Mix honey with about half a gallon of hot water, bring to boil and boil for two minutes. Turn into polythene pail containing petals. Add citric acid, tea and make up to one gallon with boiling water. Add extra *1 pint* of boiling water to make up for space occupied by petals.

Allow mixture to cool to approximately 65°f. and add yeast and nutrient.

Cover as for beers and ferment in warm place for five-six days.

Strain out flowers and return strained liquor to fermenting vessel. Cover as before and ferment for further five-six days. Thereafter proceed as for CLOVER MEAD on page 137.

ELDERFLOWER MEAD

4 lb. honey · ¼ oz. citric acid
¼ pint strong freshly-made tea
1 pint elderflowers · yeast · nutrient

No extra water is needed in this recipe as the flowers occupy so little space.

Mix honey with about half a gallon of hot water, bring slowly to the boil and boil for two minutes. Turn into polythene pail containing flowers.

Add citric acid and tea and make up to one gallon with boiling water.

Allow mixture to cool to 65°F. and add yeast and nutrient.

Thereafter proceed as for CLOVER MEAD on page 137.

HAWTHORN (MAY-FLOWER) MEAD

4 lb. honey · ¼ oz. citric acid
¼ pint freshly made strong tea
1 pint hawthorn flowers · yeast · nutrient

No extra water need be added in this recipe as the flowers occupy so little space.

Mix honey with about half gallon of hot water, bring to the boil and boil for two minutes. Turn into polythene pail containing flowers, add citric acid and tea and make up to one gallon with boiling water.

Allow to cool to approximately 65°F. and add yeast and nutrient. Thereafter proceed as for CLOVER MEAD on page 137.

12

Some Questions and Answers

Draught Beer Man

In all the recipes you have sent me and in all the little odd pieces I have read here and there, bottling the finished beer is recommended. I am a draught beer man and so are my three sons. Between us we put down nigh on a gallon each night including one pint for my wife. Emptying bottles at this rate is great fun, but filling them is another matter. Can we use gallon stone jars with taps fitted to do away with all this bottling?

As you are a draught beer man, there is no need to bottle your beer especially as so much is used up in so little time. By all means use gallon size stone jars – or larger ones if you want to. If we here used as much beer in so little time we would use two-gallon or even four-gallon jars; after all, in draught beer there is no froth or gaseousness to be lost, and I doubt if there would be any noticeable loss of quality in the last few pints to be drawn off when only a few days have elapsed since the jar was originally opened.

If it were a matter of a week or more from tapping to the final pint being drawn, there would be good deal less quality in the last pint or two.

Liquorice Sticks

I have been using liquorice sticks in a few beers and like the result of this. Would you say they would improve all beers?

Only you can answer that one. If you think you would like the result of using liquorice in all your beers, there is no earthly reason for not doing so. Personally, I cannot imagine a lager or light ale type with liquorice in it, but if you are making the darker beer and are not making lagers or light ales, then use liquorice in all of them. If you don't like it in one or two particular brews, all you have to do is leave it out next time.

Using Yeast Deposit from Commercial Beers

I understand how to obtain yeast deposit from bottled beers, but can you tell me which bottled beers are best for obtaining yeast? And can you tell me why some bottled beers have yeast in them while others do not?

People from various parts of the country have some success with certain bottled beers but the best for obtaining a yeast deposit for fermentation purposes are Guinness, White Label, Worthington and Red Label Bass.

The reason some bottled beers have yeast deposits and others not is that some beers, notably those brilliant, pale or light ales and lager are filtered to ensure against any risk of yeast cloud.

These beers do not contain the natural gas produced by fermentation; they are first made as draught beers; they are then filtered to brilliance, pasteurized to destroy any stray yeast spores and then charged with gas under pressure. Hence the brilliantly clear beer free of yeast deposit and a gaseous one into the bargain.

Using Fermentation Locks

I make wines with your recipes and ferment them in jars under fermentation locks and have, incidentally, won many prizes following your methods and recipes. May I ferment my beers in jars in the same way once the vigorous ferment has died down?

Of course. Many people do this with excellent results. Readers of this book may read about the use of the fermentation lock on page 35.

Top or Bottom Yeast

I have been using top fermenting yeast for some beers and bottom fermenting kinds for others. The quality of the beers seems to be the same so there is little difference in the yeasts themselves. Now I am wondering why some people recommend bottom fermenting yeast while others swear by top fermenting sorts.

I use both sorts, a bottom fermenting kind for pale beers for I find that clearer beer results more quickly; but where speed of clearing, as when draught beers are being made, is not important, I use a top fermenting yeast. Either way, one still gets a deposit – though less when a top ferment is used.

People often find it advantageous to use a bottom ferment when a rather smaller fermenting vessel than is actually needed is in use as these do not produce so much top yeast; therefore, not quite so much head room is needed. Like yourself, I have found no actual difference in the qualities of the different beers made with the two different types of yeast.

One Gallon in a Two Gallon Jar

All my wine fermenting jars hold two gallons. Now that I am starting to make beers as well as wines I would like to make one gallon at a time until I feel confident enough to make larger amounts. I would like to ferment one gallon of beer in a two gallon jar; is there any reason for not doing this?

No reason at all. But do not put your beers into jars until the vigorous ferment has died down and then siphon it into the jar so that less yeast comes over than if it were poured. I advise this as if too much yeast goes into the jar, there is likely to be a very vigorous ferment after the airing given by siphoning. If this happened, the yeast would probably force itself up through the fermentation lock, down the side of the jar and on to any surface the jar might be standing on. I'd use a tap jar if you have one so that when fermentation has ceased, the yeast will settle below the tap. This will allow all but the first half pint to be drained off clear. You may either leave the lock in place when the beer is being drawn off, in which case the lock will work in reverse as beer comes out and air is drawn in. Otherwise, remove the lock from the bung and insert a spile – see BREWING VOCABULARY, page 152. The spile must be removed to allow air into the jar as beer is drawn otherwise the beer will not run.

Clearing Beer

I have been told that if a little powdered gelatine is used in all recipes clearing is very rapid. My friend dissolved half an ounce in warm water and adds this to four gallons before adding yeast.

You can do this if you want to, but I find it best to let the beer clear itself. Then, if it is a bit slower than usual, clarify with gelatine or isinglass.

Very Bitter Bitter

I am a draught bitter fan and my day is not complete if I do not have my three pints an evening. I have found in the recipes you sent me that when using more hops to get more bitterness, I have to use more malt to balance this. Would using more hops produce the bitterness and would leaving out the extra malt spoil the beer?

In the ordinary way, if a lot of hops are used more malt is needed to balance the bitterness otherwise the beer might be too bitter for some people. But if you want a very bitter bitter, the answer would be to use more hops and not to add more malt to balance them.

This is a matter of absolute trial and error because only you know how bitter you want your bitter. Make one gallon lots until you get what you want, then make larger amounts.

Too Much Froth

Having been making sparkling (frothy) beers for some time quite successfully, I am puzzled by a recent happening. I am certain my hydrometer readings were accurate and that I primed with the right amount of sugar to give the usual amount of gas into the beer, as always; but for some reason, on opening the first bottle of my most recent batch there was what I can only describe a one almighty fountain of foam. In fact, it would have made an admirable fire extinguisher. This subsided quite quickly, but I lost about a quarter pint from the quart bottle. The other bottle from the same batch acted similarly, but these I unscrewed very carefully and very little so as to let off the gas without losing more than a few drops of beer from each bottle, tightening the stoppers as soon as fizzing stopped. What I would like to know is, could hot weather have caused this?

Hot weather certainly will have this affect if the beers are stored in a place that is affected by hot weather. It was not caused by more gas than expected being formed, as some people may have imagined. What happened was that warmth penetrated the beer and expanded it, or, in other words, increased its volume – or made slightly more of it, as it were. This expansion compressed the gas between the beer and the stopper into perhaps as little as half the space it would have had if this expansion had not taken place. The same thing happens with fully fermented wines, where there has been no secondary fermentation in the bottle. In this case, when the seal is broken, the cork pops out and dances from ceiling to wall. In both cases there is nothing to worry about. No wine is lost and only a very little beer. A cool place for storage, if this is possible, will prevent this happening.

Too Many Recipes

So far I have collected seven recipes for brown ale. All are different in one way or another, and what worries me is how can each be called a brown ale recipe. Anyway, can you please tell me which is the best to use?

You really ought not to collect recipes; it never makes choosing the right one easier. The fact is that all the recipes you sent along will make brown ale. The fact that each resulting ale will differ slightly from the last, and the next for that matter, is only natural. Each commercial brewer makes his brown ale different from his competitor's; thus one group of people swear by so-and-so's 'Brown', while another group swears by someone else's.

As for choosing the right one for you to use is like asking me to choose a wife for you; only you know what you want, and because you have so many recipes for the one type of ale it is going to be harder to choose the right one than if you had only two or three.

Mixed Method

I have made beers for a long time (very quietly of course, owing to the Excise regulations that used to be in force) and I have used grain malts and malt extracts separately. Both beers are good, but I feel that if I used the mashing method with grain malts as I have done all along and then add say a pound of malt extract after boiling, or some time before the yeast is added, I would get an even better beer. Would you let me have your opinion on this.

Many amateurs do this with most excellent results, but beginners might find it a little confusing. Do take into account that the malt extract contains a certain amount of sugar. But if you use the hydrometer you can account for this.

Flowers for Wines

I have been very successful in making flower wines using the flowers of dandelions, rose petals, hawthorn, elderflowers etc. Now I would like to use bluebells, lilac, buttercups and other wild flowers that abound in this area, but I have no idea how much of each kind of flower to use.

Don't use any of these flowers. It is most important to stress that some flowers are suitable while others are not. Recipes for using suitable flowers are plentiful, and I'm sorry to say a few recipes for using flowers that can produce poisonous potions are also available. Readers of this book are perfectly safe in using the flowers in the recipes here. On no account try using other flowers. To list all those unsuitable would be difficult indeed – so stick to those known to be perfectly safe and indeed wholesome.

Cracking Grain Malts

I have very much enjoyed your book, and my first batches of beer using malt extracts have been very good. However, I do have one question to ask you. What is the best method of cracking grain malts?

The best method of cracking malt is to go over it with an ordinary rolling pin. The grain should be very lightly cracked. (You can avoid using grain malts altogether and get good results by using malts in either dried or syrup form.)

Brewing Vocabulary

BLACK (*or* GREEN) TREACLE A dark molasses. It is strongly flavoured, so use very little of it.

BLACK MALT A malt that has been roasted only very slightly less than patent black malt.

BOTTOMS *See* Lees.

CARAMEL Burnt sugar.

CARAMELIZED MALT EXTRACT Malt extract flavoured slightly with caramel. It may be obtained in syrup or dried form.

CRYSTAL MALT In this type of malt, the interior of the grain has a brown, vitreous appearance. In most recipes calling for crystal malt, pale malt may be used, except when a very fine and subtle difference in flavour is required.

CYTASE The enzyme in grain barley which dissolves the cellulose skin, thus allowing digestive ferments to take place in the grain.

DEMERARA SUGAR Ordinary brown sugar, not too highly flavoured.

DEXTRINS Essential substances found in wort during mashing.

DIASTASE An enzyme in grain barley which converts starch to fermentable sugars.

FINED Having been heated with isinglass or other clarifying medium.

FININGS Isinglass or other clarifying mediums.

FLAKED MAIZE Corn flakes before being processed as a breakfast cereal.

GOLDEN SYRUP A pale golden molasses with very little flavour.

GOODS Barley having been malted and crushed and ready for the mash tun.

GREEN BARLEY Barley germinated — malted — but not yet dried in the kiln.

GRIST Goods (as above), but already in the mash tun.

GRIT Term used to denote grain other than barley sometimes used in brewing.

GYPSUM Material contained in most water-treatment substances. An essential ingredient of water, or brewery liquor.

HEAD That lovely stuff we have on the top of beers.

HEADING LIQUID Liquid supplied by home-brew firms to give artificial head to beers.

HOP BAG Bag used when hops are to be kept separate from the brew so that they may be removed in 'the bag'.

INVERT SUGAR *See* Appendix

LACTOSE Milk sugar used for sweetening stouts—(and other beers where necessary, but generally stouts) hence the once-popular Milk Stout.

LEES Sediment made up of dead yeast cells and other matter in the fermenting vessel.

LIGHT DRIED MALT EXTRACT A malt that has been dried after being extracted from the grain. It may be used instead of pale or crystal malt.

MALT Strictly, malt still in the grain of uncrushed malted barley—otherwise 'grain malt'.

MALTED BARLEY Barley with the malt still in the grain. You can learn to toast or roast it under a grill to obtain the required effect—pale, medium, dark, very dark, and so on.

MALT EXTRACT Extract of malt as a liquid in tins. Also supplied dry as a powder. In the United States available at drug stores in the form of syrups. They are classified as extra pale, light, and dark. They are suitable for use with recipes calling for light, pale, and dark malt extract.

MALTOSE The all-important fermentable sugar produced during malting.

NUTRIENT Chemical matter (nitrogenous) added to wines and worts to assist yeast reproduction.

PALE DRIED MALT EXTRACT This is usually the best type of pale dried malt to use for lighter beers, but a pale malt extract (malt extracted from lightly roasted grain) may be substituted for it.

PALE MALT *See* Crystal malt.

PATENT BLACK MALT The very darkly roasted malt.

POLISHING Producing brilliance in beers by filtering.

ROASTED MALT This usually refers to a malt roasted to a slightly darker colour and, therefore, having a slightly stronger flavour than pale or crystal malt. All malts are roasted; it is the extent and the method of roasting that make the difference in the colour of the malt and the flavour it imparts to the beer.

SHIVE—CHIVE Bored wooden plug for fitting to barrel.

SPILE Often mistakenly called 'Chive'. Small tapered wooden peg made to fit hole in *Chive*—above. Spile is removed to admit air as beer is drawn off. Must be returned firmly as soon as possible.

STILLION Wooden bed or cradle for barrel. An essential where barrels are used, otherwise weight of beer would cause the barrel staves to 'give' causing the barrel to 'weep', lose beer.

TREACLE Molasses.

WEEPING BARREL Barrel leaking owing to staves having given way.

Appendix

The following is a list of firms where the various materials and ingredients mentioned in this book may be obtained:

Berg & Sons, 511 Puyallup Avenue, Tacoma 2, Wash.
Wine Art, P.O. Box 2701, Vancouver 3, B.C., Canada
Party House Beverage, 10420 16th Ave. S.W., White Center, Wash.
Aetna Bottle Co., 708 Rainier Ave. South, Seattle 44, Wash.

Milan Laboratory, 57 Spring Street, New York, N.Y.
Semplex, Box 7208, Minneapolis, Minn.

INVERT SUGAR—This can be made at home by the reader if he has difficulty obtaining same: Put 8 lbs. of ordinary household sugar (white sugar) in a suitable pan with 2 pints of water and ½ ounce of citric acid (obtainable in drugstores), or use the juice of four lemons. Bring slowly to a boil, stirring all the time so that all sugar dissolves. When all sugar is dissolved, allow to boil for half an hour *very* gently without stirring—or stirring only occasionally. Allow this to cool somewhat and then make up to exactly 1 gallon by adding boiled water. You now have INVERT SUGAR—the inversion being caused by the acid. To measure, use 1 pint to each 1 lb. of sugar called for in the recipe—1 pint is equal to 1 lb. of sugar. Store in suitable jars, tightly corked.

If you do not want to go to the trouble of making your own invert sugar, a very close substitute—in fact, practically identical to invert sugar—is corn sugar, classified as cereulose-dextrose.

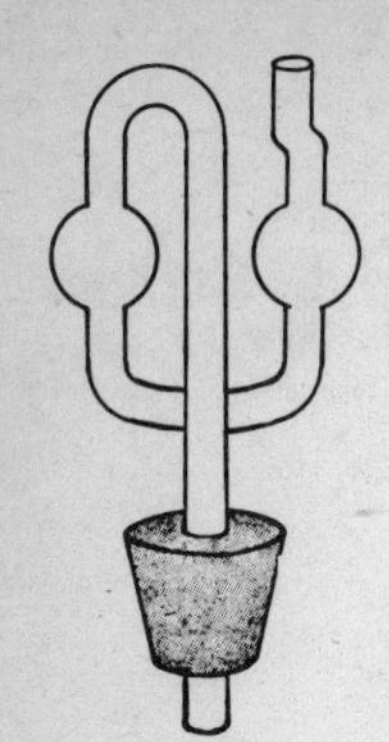

a. Cork fitted to the lock. Note that the long end of the lock is pushed through the cork.

1. Fitting the fermentation lock.

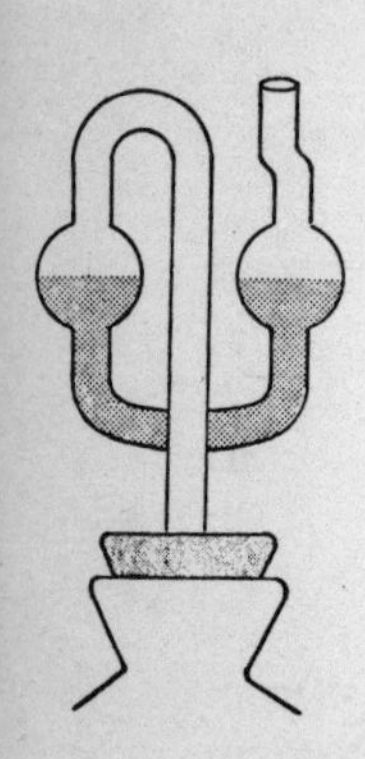

b. When the cork has been fitted to the jar, water is poured in to the level shown.

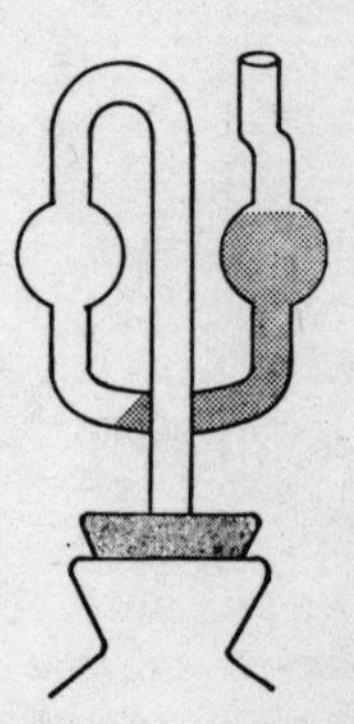

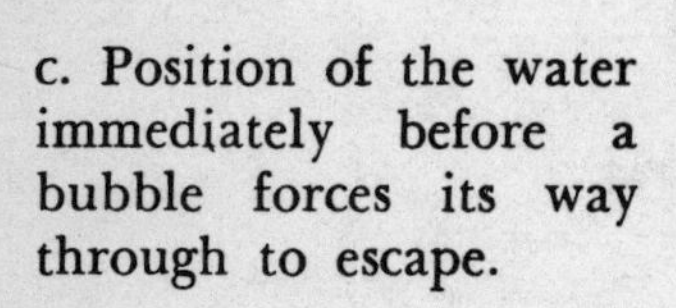

c. Position of the water immediately before a bubble forces its way through to escape.

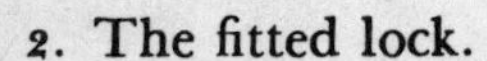

2. The fitted lock.

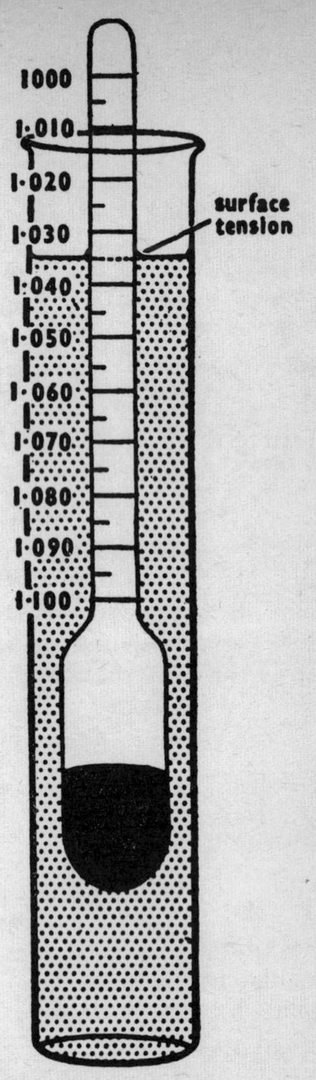

3. The Hydrometer, showing how to allow for surface tension.

Index